Vocabulary and Spelling Book

McDougal Littell

GRADE EIGHT

 **McDougal Littell**
A HOUGHTON MIFFLIN COMPANY
Evanston, Illinois   Boston   Dallas

ISBN 0-618-13669–X

10 11 12 – MDO –10 09 08 07 06

Contents

Academic Vocabulary Lessons (continued)

Spelling Lessons

Vocabulary

Vocabulary Lessons

Tools for Vocabulary Study

The *Vocabulary and Spelling Book* contains lessons designed to help you understand and remember important vocabulary skills and strategies. You will often need to use basic reference sources to master these new techniques and to complete the exercises within the book. Use the information below to help you in your work.

Using References

Dictionaries

A **dictionary** can tell you more than just the meanings of words. For example, look at the information you can learn from the entries below.

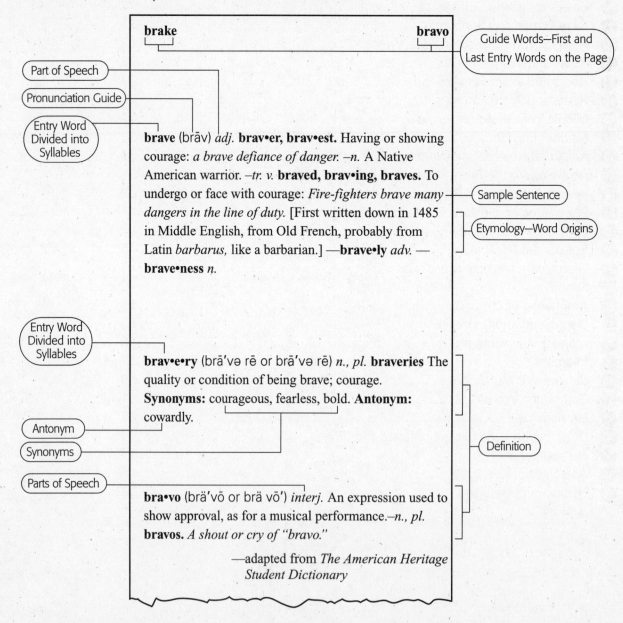

brake   **bravo**

Guide Words—First and Last Entry Words on the Page

Part of Speech

Pronunciation Guide

Entry Word Divided into Syllables

brave (brāv) *adj.* **brav•er, brav•est.** Having or showing courage: *a brave defiance of danger.* *–n.* A Native American warrior. *–tr. v.* **braved, brav•ing, braves.** To undergo or face with courage: *Fire-fighters brave many dangers in the line of duty.* [First written down in 1485 in Middle English, from Old French, probably from Latin *barbarus,* like a barbarian.] —**brave•ly** *adv.* —**brave•ness** *n.*

Sample Sentence

Etymology—Word Origins

Entry Word Divided into Syllables

brav•e•ry (brā′və rē or brā′və rē) *n., pl.* **braveries** The quality or condition of being brave; courage. **Synonyms:** courageous, fearless, bold. **Antonym:** cowardly.

Antonym

Synonyms

Definition

Parts of Speech

bra•vo (brä′vō or brä vō′) *interj.* An expression used to show approval, as for a musical performance. *–n., pl.* **bravos.** *A shout or cry of "bravo."*

—adapted from *The American Heritage Student Dictionary*

Dictionaries frequently list several definitions for the same word. How do you know which definition is the right one for your purposes?

> ### (Here's How)
>
> **Choosing the Right Definition**
>
> **1.** Read through all the definitions in the dictionary entry.
>
> **2.** Rule our any that don't make sense, given what you're reading about. If you're reading about firefighters rescuing someone, you should probably eliminate from consideration the second definition.
>
> **3.** Determine the word's part of speech in the sentence. In "The brave firefighter rescued the child," *brave* is an adjective, so you should choose the adjective definition. In "The brave began the ritual," *brave* is a noun, so you should choose the noun definition.
>
> **4.** When there's more than one definition for a particular part of speech, use synonyms in place of the word to see which meaning of the word makes the most sense in the sentence.

Thesauruses

A **thesaurus** is a dictionary of **synonyms**—words that have similar meanings. Many thesaurus entries also note **antonyms**—words that have the opposite meaning—of the entry word.

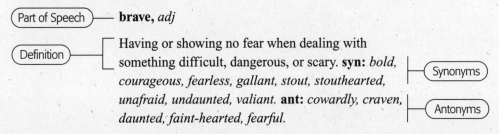

(Part of Speech)—— **brave,** *adj*

(Definition)——⌐ Having or showing no fear when dealing with
└ something difficult, dangerous, or scary. **syn:** *bold,* ┐
courageous, fearless, gallant, stout, stouthearted, ├—(Synonyms)
unafraid, undaunted, valiant. **ant:** *cowardly, craven,* ┐
daunted, faint-hearted, fearful. ├—(Antonyms)

Not all synonyms can be substituted for each other. Some words are used only in certain ways. For example, although *convey* and *transport* have similar meanings, you wouldn't ask "Did I transport what I meant here?"

Name _____ Date _____

Context Clues *Teaching*

You can sometimes tell the meaning of an unfamiliar word by looking closely at nearby words and phrases. Read the following sentence:

> He was so brazen that he would come late to class noisily, winking and grinning at all his friends.

You can infer from the context phrases - "late to class noisily" and "winking and grinning" — that *brazen* means "bold" or "shameless."

A. Context Clues in Action

In each sentence below, underline any context clues that help you figure out the meaning of the word in italics. Then write the meaning of the word.

1. Taking a slow, deep breath, I fought back an *impulse* to say something nasty to the rude official.

   meaning: _____

2. Using his *intuition* rather than his reason, the detective located the suspect.

   meaning: _____

3. Dr. Wu fears that the weak and seriously ill patient might *lapse* into a coma.

   meaning: _____

4. Sitting all alone I fell into a *reverie*, imagining all the things I wanted to do someday.

   meaning: _____

5. The shortstop *deftly* caught the fly ball and zipped it to first base.

   meaning: _____

6. Can you imagine anything more *tedious* than doing the same dull job over and over?

   meaning: _____

7. The more I stretch and exercise, the more *flexible* my joints become.

   meaning: _____

8. When we saw a blinking red light and a man waving a flag, we realized there was some kind of *hazard* ahead.

   meaning: _____

9. If that tree falls across the road, it will *obstruct* traffic in and out of the area.

   meaning: _____

10. There was something *sinister* about the dark castle, with the wolves howling in the distance.

   meaning: _____

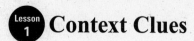

Context Clues

More Practice

impulse	*intuition*	*lapse*	*reverie*	*obstruct*
deftly	*tedious*	*flexible*	*hazard*	*sinister*

B. Vocabulary Words in Action

Review the meanings of the words in the list above. Then insert in each sentence
the word that correctly fits the meaning.

1. The archer made a curved bow from a _____ piece of sapling.

2. My _____ told me that the cat would not like the new puppy.

3. Several cars skidded on the ice past the _____ lights.

4. Acting on _____, the spy leaped away from the car as it exploded.

5. Carl thought mowing the lawn was the most _____ chore ever.

6. In court the defendant would start to explain and then _____ into silence.

7. The weaver _____ worked the colorful threads through the loom.

8. Don't interrupt Grandpa in his _____ about playing major league ball.

9. Loss of important evidence will _____ the progress of the investigation.

10. There were warnings of a _____ plot to take over the government of the tiny republic.

C. Vocabulary Challenge

Look at the following words and their meanings. Then for each word write a
sentence that uses the word and includes a context clue to its meaning.

1. **console**   give comfort to; express sympathy for

_____

2. **munitions** weapons and ammunition

_____

3. **elated**   proud and joyful

_____

4. **prosperous** successful; well-to-do

_____

5. **minimal**   small in amount; only barely adequate

_____

Restatement and Example Clues

Lesson 2

Teaching

A writer may provide context clues by restating a term in easier language. Commas, dashes, or other punctuation can point to a restatement clue, along with expressions such as *that is, in other words,* and *or.*

My father is a podiatrist, **or foot doctor**.

The **restatement clue**, "or foot doctor," tells you the meaning of *podiatrist*.

Another way writers can suggest the meanings of words is to give one or two **examples,** as in the following sentence:

Fred showed some very **belligerent** traits, such as shouting at other drivers and constantly getting into fights.

The examples suggest that *belligerent* means something like "hostile" or "bad-tempered."

A. Restatement and Example Clues in Action

In each sentence below, first look at the italicized word, then look for clues to its meaning. Circle either *restatement* or *example.* Then write a meaning for the italicized word.

1. Mano had such a *longing* for the horse that he knew he would never want anything so much again.
   restatement/example

   meaning: _____

2. The burning of the our home was a *calamity*—a real disaster.
   restatement/example

   meaning: _____

3. *Impediments* to his getting the job included his youth and inexperience and his lack of language skills.
   restatement/example

   meaning: _____

4. When using power tools you should take *precautions*, such as wearing safety goggles and treating the equipment properly.
   restatement/example

   meaning: _____

5. We feared lightning would *ignite* the dry grass and burn up the fields.
   restatement/example

   meaning: _____

6. The legend told of a *pauper*, or person without wealth, who dreamed of owning a horse.
   restatement/example

   meaning: _____

7. The *precipitation* we expect this weekend may come in the form of rain, sleet, or snow.
   restatement/example

   meaning: _____

8. The judge's sentence was *punitive*; that is, it was meant to punish the offender.
   restatement/example

   meaning: _____

9. Unfortunately, this diamond has some *flaws*, including a yellow color and a cloudy appearance.
   restatement/example

   meaning: _____

10. The man was *infuriated*: he simply flew into a rage.
    restatement/example

    meaning: _____

Restatement and Example Clues

More Practice

| longing | calamity | punitive | precautions | impediment |
| ignite | pauper | infuriated | flaws | precipitation |

B. Vocabulary Words in Action

Review the meanings of the words in the list above. Then insert in each sentence the word that correctly fits the meaning.

1. Your argument is fairly good, but there are some _____ in it.

2. All day I had a strong _____, or desire, for a piece of chocolate cake.

3. The crop should be in good shape this year if we get enough _____.

4. Stored gasoline and a stray match helped _____ the warehouse, which was soon in flames.

5. Jason felt it was a _____ —a disaster—when he got B's on his two tests.

6. The fantasy was about a _____ who became rich through a magic fish.

7. Bad study habits can be an _____ to your success.

8. In dealing with the uprising, the government was forced to take _____ measures.

9. Take extra _____ if the roads are slippery.

10. When she discovered the broken vase, Alice became _____.

C. Vocabulary Challenge

Look at the following words and their meanings. Then for each word write a sentence that uses the word and includes a context clue to its meaning.

1. **taunted**   teased

_____

2. **ailment**   illness

_____

3. **clamor**   loud noise

_____

4. **consequence**   result

_____

5. **impartial**   fair, unbiased

_____

Definition and Example Clues

Lesson 3

Two forms of context clues are example(s) and definition of an unfamiliar word. Read the sentences below.

We collected **kindling**, such as dry twigs and branches, to start the fire.

The **examples,** "such as dry twigs and branches" tell you that *kindling* means "easily burned materials used to start a fire." The terms *like, such as, for example,* and *other* often signal an example format.

A **dirigible** is an aircraft that is lighter than air.

A **definition clue** is usually signaled by a form of the verb *to be* (*am, is, are, was, were*) or by commas or dashes. Often a definition clue tells what class the item is in (aircraft) and then tells how it is different from other members of that class (lighter than air).

A. Definition and Example Clues in Action

In each sentence below, first look at the italicized word, then look for clues to its meaning. Circle either **example** or **definition**. Then write a meaning for the italicized word.

1. The prisoner was in a state of *wrath*—a feeling of intense anger.
example/definition

   meaning: _____

2. I liked his *blunt* manner—for example, he always told me the truth.
example/definition

   meaning: _____

3. To *shun* someone is to have nothing to do with that person.
example/definition

   meaning: _____

4. The rain was *consistent*—that is, it kept the same rhythm and intensity for more than an hour.
example/definition

   meaning: _____

5. Afterward Jerry showed some signs *of remorse,* such as apologizing to everyone and paying back the money he had lost.
example/definition

   meaning: _____

6. She had *a gaudy* wardrobe—for example, pink shoes, bright hats, and sweaters with rhinestones.
example/definition

   meaning: _____

7. I think you should be *skeptical* about those claims. That is, you should doubt or question them first.
example/definition

   meaning: _____

8. As spring approached we began to see new *hues* in the landscape, such as various shades of green, yellow, and gold.
example/definition

   meaning: _____

9. One kind of *phobia* is a fear of flying. There are other kinds, such as a fear of insects and a fear of high places.
example/definition

   meaning: _____

10. He seemed to be ill, but it was merely a *ruse,* that is, a clever trick to deceive us.
example/definition

    meaning: _____

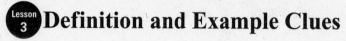

Definition and Example Clues

Lesson 3

More Practice

ruse	*blunt*	*phobia*	*consistent*	*shun*
wrath	*gaudy*	*remorse*	*skeptical*	*hues*

B. Vocabulary Words in Action

Review the meanings of the words in the list above. Then insert in each sentence
the word that correctly fits the meaning.

1. Tim was really embarrassed; his face showed _____ from pink to scarlet.

2. His _____ clothes were out of place at the funeral.

3. The suspect's story was not _____ with what the evidence showed.

4. The teacher was quite _____ about Ed's story. She didn't see how it could be true.

5. The mayor has a _____ manner—rather plain-spoken and abrupt.

6. He refused to enter that small, enclosed space. He must have had some kind of _____ about it.

7. The tiger was in quite a state of _____—snarling, snapping, and lunging at the keeper.

8. Fortunately, the general thought of a clever _____ that completely fooled the enemy.

9. _____ is an emotion we don't always see in convicted criminals, but Jones seemed to be really sorry.

10. My friends all began to _____ me until they realized I had never given away the secret

C. Vocabulary Challenge

Look at the following words and their meanings. Then for each word write a
sentence that uses the word and includes a context clue to its meaning.

1. **morsel**   small bite or portion of food

   _____

2. **jovial**   full of hearty good humor

   _____

3. **languish**   become weak; fail in health

   _____

4. **wary**   cautious; on one's guard

   _____

5. **allege**   declare, especially without proof

   _____

Comparison and Contrast Clues

Lesson 4

Sometime you can tell the meaning of an unfamiliar word when it is compared or contrasted to something familiar. Context clues that show **comparison** include *like, as, similar,* and *in the same way.* **Contrasts** may be signaled by words such as *but, although, however,* and *on the other hand.*

> Kari's happy face was *luminous,* **like** the rays of the sun.

The clue word *like* in this sentence tells you that *luminous* means "shining" or "giving off light."

> I assumed a rhino would move in a *lumbering* manner, **but** it raced across the screen like an attacking army tank.

The clue word **but** in this sentence suggests that *lumbering* means "moving in a heavy, slow manner."

A. Comparison and Contrast Clues in Action

Read the following sentences and underline each word or phrase that signals a comparison or contrast clue. Circle **comparison** or **contrast,** depending on the clue. Then write the meaning of each italicized word.

1. The sink was *clogged,* like a ball stuck in the vacuum cleaner.
   comparison/contrast

   meaning: _____

2. The meeting was held in the main house, but refreshments were served in the *annex.*
   comparison/contrast

   meaning: _____

3. We thought we were seeing the real painting, but it turned out to be a *fraud.*
   comparison/contrast

   meaning: _____

4. Although we had expected a *multitude* to come to the rally, only ten or fifteen people showed up.
   comparison/contrast

   meaning: _____

5. That faucet is *faulty,* just like all the other things in this house that don't work.
   comparison/contrast

   meaning: _____

6. The summer was *sultry;* on the other hand, the fall was cool and dry.
   comparison/contrast

   meaning: _____

7. The moon will *diminish* in size at the end of the month; however, it will grow during the first part of the month.
   comparison/contrast

   meaning: _____

8. When the winner was announced, there was *pandemonium* in the hall, something like what happens in the final seconds of a close basketball game.
   comparison/contrast

   meaning: _____

9. The coach's *empathy* for her team was like that of a mother for her children.
   comparison/contrast

   meaning: _____

10. I like foods that are hot and spicy, but my brother's diet is much more *bland.*
    comparison/contrast

    meaning: _____

Comparison and Contrast Clues

More Practice

clogged	annex	bland	fraud	multitude
faulty	empathy	sultry	diminish	pandemonium

B. Vocabulary Words in Action

Review the meanings of the words in the list above. Then insert in each sentence the word that correctly fits the meaning.

1. The toaster is still working, even though the microwave is _____.

2. The next morning a quiet mood settled over the city, unlike the _____ of the night before.

3. The _____ weather made me feel like I was swimming in warm water.

4. Although only a few flowers were growing in the valley, we could see a _____ of them on the hill.

5. The bathroom pipe was _____; however, the kitchen drain was open and clear.

6. This soup is just as _____ as some of the other unexciting dishes we've been having lately.

7. We had hoped for _____, but we were treated mostly with hostility and distrust.

8. The building has an _____ that reminds me of the new bedroom over the garage.

9. _____ is regarded as a crime in the same way as other dishonest business deals are.

10. I was afraid of snowboarding at first, but once I tried it, my fears began to _____.

C. Vocabulary Challenge

Look at the following words and their meanings. Then for each word write a sentence that uses the word and includes a context clue to its meaning.

1. **hilarious**   very funny; noisily merry

   _____

2. **ordeal**   a difficult or painful experience

   _____

3. **serene**   calm, tranquil, peaceful

   _____

4. **renovate**   repair; restore to an earlier condition

   _____

5. **malice**   a desire to hurt others; ill will

   _____

General Context Clues   *Teaching*

You can often tell the meaning of an unfamiliar word by looking closely at words and phrases in the same sentence or nearby sentences. Read the following passage:

> Listeners were shocked by the speaker's **diatribe.** They hadn't expected such harsh words against the mayor.

You can infer from the context words and phrases "Listeners were shocked", and "harsh words against the mayor" that *diatribe* means a strongly worded, even abusive, criticism.

A. Using General Context Clues in Action

Read the following sentences and underline any word or phrase that signals a context clue for each italicized word. Then write the meaning for each italicized word.

1. The odor *pervaded* the building. After awhile no resident on any floor could escape it.

   meaning: _____

2. The dog crept slowly closer, doing it so *surreptitiously* that the cat got quite a surprise.

   meaning: _____

3. I'd like to *collaborate* with you on the science project. I think we each would have something to contribute.

   meaning: _____

4. I always thought he was my friend. I realized I was wrong when he started making those *derogatory* comments about me.

   meaning: _____

5. My father respects hard work. I know he will *commend* me for painting the entire garage.

   meaning: _____

6. The *impudent* child ran into the room. The first thing he did was stick out his tongue at the teacher.

   meaning: _____

7. The week-old fruit really wasn't *palatable*. I had to spit it out.

   meaning: _____

8. The *ransom* note came in the mail. It demanded three million dollars for the return of the jewels.

   meaning: _____

9. Your offer of money was very *liberal*. I must say it was much more than I expected.

   meaning: _____

10. The new neighbors must be pretty *affluent*. They own three expensive cars and a boat.

   meaning: _____

General Context Clues

More Practice

pervaded	surreptitiously	collaborate	commend	impudent
palatable	ransom	liberal	derogatory	affluent

B. Vocabulary Words in Action

Review the meanings of the words in the list above. Then insert in each sentence
the word that correctly fits the meaning.

1. The _____ demand told the detectives where to drop the money.

2. The meal was barely _____. By that time, though, I was so hungry that I ate it anyway.

3. You spoke really rudely to her. Don't you think you were being a little _____?

4. We may not be as _____ as some. On the other hand, we've always made do.

5. Sasha and I want to give a surprise party and _____ on the arrangements.

6. Dad poured a _____ amount of barbecue sauce on the steaks. I guess he knows how
   much we like the stuff!

7. A sense of menace _____ the house. We could feel it everywhere we went.

8. I don't mean this in any _____ way, but I think you should be a little more careful about
   what you say.

9. I want to _____ you on your report about whales in class. It was the best you've done
   all year.

10. The spy inched _____ along the prison wall. He was afraid he'd be seen in the floodlights.

C. Vocabulary Challenge

Look at the following words and their meanings. Then for each word write a
sentence that uses the word and includes a context clue to its meaning.

1. **stealthy**   acting in a quiet, cautious way

   _____

2. **elude**   escape from

   _____

3. **deleterious** having a harmful effect; injurious

   _____

4. **apparition** a ghostly figure; a specter

   _____

5. **gregarious** seeking and enjoying the company of others

   _____

Lesson 6 Prefixes and Base Words

Teaching

Often you can figure out the meaning of a word by breaking it into parts and then looking at the meaning of each part. One kind of word part is a **prefix,** which can be attached to the beginning of a word. A **base word** is a word that can stand alone. Look at the examples below.

inaudible   **reunite**

The prefix *in-* means "not." The base word *audible* means "able to be heard." Thus, the word *inaudible* means "not able to be heard." The prefix *re-* means "again." The base word *unite* means "to bring together." Thus, the word *reunite* means "to bring together again." Now look at the chart below.

Prefix	Meaning	Example
dis-	not, opposite	disagree, dismount
im-, in-	not	impossible, inactive
mis-	wrong, not	miscount, misbehave
re-	carry, back	recook, resale
sub-	under, below	submarine, subway
super-	above, beyond	superpower, supernatural
trans-	across	transplant, transatlantic
un-	not	uncertain, unconscious

A. Prefixes and Base Words in Action

For each example in Column A, draw a line between the prefix and the base word. Then match each example with its correct meaning in Column B by writing the letter in the blank. Use a dictionary if necessary.

Column A

1. misfortune _____
2. indelicate _____
3. unfounded _____
4. recycle _____
5. dishonest _____
6. immature _____
7. transcontinental _____
8. supersonic _____
9. unsettled _____
10. subsoil _____

Column B

A. not in order

B. bad luck

C. to use again

D. offensive or in bad taste

E. from coast to coast

F. faster than the speed of sound

G. childish

H. layer of earth below the surface

I. not truthful

J. not based on fact or evidence

Lesson 6 **Prefixes and Base Words**

More Practice

B. Vocabulary in Action

Circle ten words that begin with the prefixes *dis-*, *im-/in-*, *mis-*, *re-*, and *un-* in the passage below. Then write a prediction of each example's meaning. Use your knowledge of word parts and context clues to figure out what the words mean.

"Halt! snorted the dragon as he uncurled himself from his nap. "How dare you dishonor my home?" Will, a bold knight, declared "I will dislodge you from this place and rearrange your features with my fists." "You incompetent twit," roared the dragon. "Do you not know that I am immortal? You cannot kill me, though you may dislocate my shoulder if you are very strong. Then, after I've conquered you I will have you for dinner, either boiled or uncooked, it's all the same to me." "Perhaps I've misjudged you, sir" stammered Will the Bold. "I will readjust my plans and perhaps come to fight you another day."

	Prefix	Base word	Meaning
1.	_____	_____	_____
2.	_____	_____	_____
3.	_____	_____	_____
4.	_____	_____	_____
5.	_____	_____	_____
6.	_____	_____	_____
7.	_____	_____	_____
8.	_____	_____	_____
9.	_____	_____	_____
10.	_____	_____	_____

C. Vocabulary Challenge

Each prefix below can be added to the three base words provided. Circle the correct base word and write the complete word in the blank for each sentence.

1. *un-* (welcome, usual, certain) I am _____ of my performance on yesterday's math test.

2. *im-* (perfect, possible, polite) The climbers found it _____ to make the summit.

3. *dis-* (respect, count, place) The new development will _____ the wetlands.

4. *mis-* (place, judge, lead) I often _____ how far I can run.

Prefixes and Base Words

Lesson 7

Teaching

Knowing how words are put together can help you figure out their meanings.
Base words—words that can stand alone—change their meaning when prefixes or
suffixes are attached to them. A **prefix** is a word part that can be attached to the
beginning of a word. Look at the examples below.

maltreatment   *irrational*

The prefix *mal-* means "bad." The word *treatment* means "handling or dealing with
something." Thus, the word *maltreatment* means "handling something badly." The
prefix *ir-* means "not." The base word *rational* means "able to reason." Thus, the
word *irrational* means "not able to reason or "not in accord with reason." Now look
at the chart below.

Prefix	Meaning	Example
anti-	against	antifreeze
hyper-	more than normal	hypertension
il-	not	illogical
inter-	between, among	interact
ir-	not	irresistible
mal-	bad	maladjusted
omni-	all	omnidirectional

A. Prefixes and Base Words in Action

For each example in Column A, draw a line between the prefix and the base word.
Then match each example with its correct meaning in Column B by writing the letter
in the blank. Use a dictionary to find the meaning of any unfamiliar base words.

Column A	Column B
1. interstate _____	A. all-powerful
2. illegal _____	B. not straight or even
3. hypersensitive _____	C. bad nourishment
4. omnipotent _____	D. unfriendly
5. malformed _____	E. against the law
6. irregular _____	F. across state lines
7. hyperventilate _____	G. hard to read
8. illegible _____	H. easily offended
9. antisocial _____	I. badly shaped
10. malnutrition _____	J. breathe too fast or deep

Lesson 7 Prefixes and Base Words

B. Vocabulary in Action

Circle ten words that begin with the prefixes *anti-, hyper-, il-, inter-, ir-, mal-,* and *omni-* in the sentences below. Then write a definition for each word, using a dictionary for assistance.

1. As the sirens sounded, the antiaircraft guns began to roar.

   meaning: _____

2. It was his irresponsible behavior that got him into trouble.

   meaning: _____

3. Over the years, inhabitants of the two villages began to intermarry.

   meaning: _____

4. My neighbors' noisy young twins are really maladjusted.

   meaning: _____

5. Stan was on antibiotics for ten days for his infection.

   meaning: _____

6. Doctors and lawyers have to worry about being sued for malpractice.

   meaning: _____

7. Sally's hyperactive little dog never seems to sit still.

   meaning: _____

8. The old man was illiterate, but wise in the ways of the world.

   meaning: _____

9. Pastor Bob tells me that the people in the town are not as irreligious as they used to be.

   meaning: _____

10. What we need is an intercity bus line so people can get to their jobs.

   meaning: _____

C. Vocabulary Challenge

Each prefix below can be added to the three base words provided. Circle the correct base word and write the complete word in the blank for each sentence.

1. *anti-* (nuclear, social, slavery) Several _____ groups helped free black Americans in the 1800s.

2. *ir-* (resolute, recoverable, revocable) The divers decided that the sunken ship was _____.

3. *inter-* (lock, play, change) Both cars are the same model, so the parts _____ with each other.

4. *anti-* (septic, theft, hero) Does your car have an _____ device?

Prefixes and Base Words

Lesson 8   *Teaching*

Whenever you see an unfamiliar word, try breaking it into its parts. If you know the meaning of the parts, you can often guess the meaning of the whole word, especially with the help of context clues. A word part that is attached to the beginning of a **base word** is called a **prefix.** Look at these examples.

deform   **semiannual**

The prefix *de-* means "make the opposite of, undo." The word *form* means "shape." Thus the word *deform* means "to undo the shape of, disfigure, make ugly." The prefix *semi* means "half." The word *annual* means "yearly." Thus, the word *semiannual* means "every half year." Now look at the chart below.

Prefix	Meaning	Example
co-	together, equally, jointly	copilot
counter-	contrary, opposite	counterpart
de-	make the opposite of	defrost
mono-	one	monotone
multi-	many	multimillionaire
post-	after	postwar
semi-	half	semicircle

A. Prefixes and Base Words in Action

For each example in Column A, draw a line between the prefix and the base word. Then match each example with its correct meaning in Column B by writing the letter in the blank. Use a dictionary to find the meaning of any unfamiliar base words.

Column A

1. postgraduate _____

2. monorail   _____

3. decontaminate _____

4. coeducation   _____

5. multimedia   _____

6. semiretired   _____

7. counterintuitive _____

8. decentralize _____

9. postoperative _____

10. semiprecious _____

Column B

A. mixing text, graphics, video, sound

B. still working part time

C. both sexes in school together

D. study after getting a degree

E. to spread out, disperse

F. not the most expensive

G. following surgery

H. to eliminate the poisons

I. against common sense

J. running on a single track

Prefixes and Base Words   *More Practice*

B. Vocabulary in Action

In the passage below, circle the ten words that begin with the prefix *co-*, *counter-*, *de-*, *mono-*, *multi-*, *post*, or *semi-*. Use your knowledge of word parts and context clues to predict what the words mean. Write the meaning of each example. Use a dictionary if you need to.

Last Friday the boss was about ready to fire half of my coworkers. "They're ignorant and uneducated," he complained. "They even talk in monosyllables!" He was really getting steamed up. I didn't want his mood to degenerate any further, so I figured I'd try to defuse the situation. "Listen, I have a counterproposal," I said. "You don't need to fire people. I know they're mostly semiskilled, but you've got some real multitalented folks here. They never had decent educational opportunities, but we could counteract that with some good training programs. After all, you don't need people here who are doing postdoctoral study, you just need workers who have the skills and knowledge they need. When that happens, they won't think that you devalue their work." The boss looked at me for a moment. Then he said, "You know, you just might have something there."

1. word: _____ meaning: _____

2. word: _____ meaning: _____

3. word: _____ meaning: _____

4. word: _____ meaning: _____

5. word: _____ meaning: _____

6. word: _____ meaning: _____

7. word: _____ meaning: _____

8. word: _____ meaning: _____

9. word: _____ meaning: _____

10. word: _____ meaning: _____

C. Vocabulary Challenge

Change each of the following base words into another word, by using one of the prefixes in this lesson. Then write a sentence that uses the new word. Use a dictionary to find the meaning of any unfamiliar base words.

1. sensitize _____

2. attack _____

3. cultural _____

4. code _____

5. formal _____

Base Words and Suffixes

Teaching

Lesson 9

Since words are often put together out of parts, knowing what the parts mean can help you figure out what the words mean. A **base word** can stand alone, but it may be combined with a prefix and/or a suffix. A **suffix** is a word part that attaches to the end of a base word, changing its meaning or its function in the sentence—that is, its part of speech. The suffixes in this lesson form adjectives and adverbs.

music + -al (like, suited for)   = musical

quiet + -ly (in a certain way)   = quietly

The suffix -al turns a noun into an adjective. The suffix -ly turns an adjective into an adverb. Read the information on the chart below.

Suffix	Part of Speech	Meaning	Example
-able/ible	adjective	able, capable	washable
-al	adjective	like, suited to	personal
-er	adjective	more (in comparison)	smarter
-est	adjective	most (in comparison)	smartest
-ful	adjective	full of	joyful
-less	adjective	without	tireless
-ly	adverb	in a(specified)way	tirelessly
-wise	adverb	in a(specified)way	lengthwise

A. Base Words and Suffixes in Action

For each example in Column A, draw a line between the base word and the suffix. Then match each example with its correct meaning in Column B. Use a dictionary if necessary.

Column A

1. worthless _____

2. agreeable _____

3. somberly _____

4. national _____

5. weakest _____

6. clockwise _____

7. smaller _____

8. thoughtful _____

9. deductible _____

10. humanely _____

Column B

A. more tiny

B. in a kind or merciful manner

C. having to do with a country

D. able to be subtracted

E. willing, pleasing

F. in a sad or gloomy way

G. without value

H. from left to right

I. serious, kind, attentive

J. easily destroyed

Lesson 9

Base Words and Suffixes

B. Vocabulary in Action

In the passage below, circle ten words that end with the suffix *-able/-ible, -al, -er/ -est, -ful, -less, -ly,* or *-wise.* Then write a prediction of each example's meaning. Use your knowledge of word parts and context clues to predict word meanings.

    Ann flew along in a bottomless swirl of clouds. She loved flying and was quite knowledgeable about it, never fearful. Sometimes she had the magical feeling that from her tiny cockpit the very stars were reachable. Then all at once the engine began to make dreadful rattling sounds and the plane slowed. Always before her craft had responded to the very light touch of her hand, but now it coughed, sputtered, and almost died. Meanwhile the force of gravity was relentless. She went through a deliberately precise instrument check, looking for what might explain the problem. When the plane fell beneath the clouds, she saw that she was over land, gliding slantwise toward the ground. When the plane's engine kicked in again and she saw the landing strip, she realized that a safe landing was now attainable. Sure enough, three minutes later she was on the ground.

1. word: _____ meaning: _____

2. word: _____ meaning: _____

3. word: _____ meaning: _____

4. word: _____ meaning: _____

5. word: _____ meaning: _____

6. word: _____ meaning: _____

7. word: _____ meaning: _____

8. word: _____ meaning: _____

9. word: _____ meaning: _____

10. word: _____ meaning: _____

C. Vocabulary Challenge

Using the suffix given, write a word that completes each sentence below.

1. *-ful* I was _____ when I heard a strange noise in my house.

2. *-ly* The cat crept _____ toward the bird.

3. *-less* She was _____ and spilled the water on the floor.

4. *-est* That was the _____ film I've seen in a long time.

5. *-er* She felt _____ after she had studied for several hours.

Name _____ Date _____

Base Words and Suffixes

Teaching

A **suffix** is a word part that is added to the end of a base word. Sometimes the spelling of the original word changes when you add the suffix. Usually, adding a suffix will change the part of speech of the base word.

Several suffixes mean "to make" and turn adjectives or nouns into verbs.

　　rational + *-ize* = rationalize "to make rational"

The suffixes *-ise-, -ate, -en,* and *-fy* also mean "to make."

Suffix	Change in Part of Speech	Meaning	Example
-ate	adjectives and nouns into verbs	to make	refrigerate
-en	adjectives and nouns into verbs	to make	harden
–fy	adjectives and nouns into verbs	to make	terrify
-ize	adjectives and nouns into verbs	to make	finalize

popularize	to make popular
orchestrate	to make ready for an orchestra
frighten	to scare, to make fearful
beautify	to make beautiful (Note: *y* changes to *i.*)

A. Suffixes in Action

Use one of the suffixes above to form a word that completes the second sentence of each pair. Change the italicized word in the first sentence into a verb.

1. Stars hold much *fascination* for me. They _____ many others too.

2. I accept your *apology.* Now _____ to your brother, too.

3. She has little *strength* since her accident. Perhaps these exercises will _____ her muscles.

4. These boots are not *tight* enough. Can we _____ the laces?

5. That statement is *false.* Do not _____ your evidence.

6. Let's have a *celebration.* I like to _____ birthdays.

7. This *summary* is too long. When you _____, remember to include only the main ideas.

8. There was no *cooperation* among the departments. Everyone has to learn to _____ or the new playground will never be completed.

9. The sky is getting *dark.* Soon it will _____ even more.

10. No one knows the *identity* of the thief. Perhaps one of the witnesses will be able to

_____ him.

Base Words and Suffixes   *More Practice*

B. Vocabulary in Action

Circle ten words that end with the suffixes *-ize, -ate, -en,* or *-fy* in the passage below. Use your knowledge of word parts and context clues to predict what the words mean. Write the meaning of each example. Use a dictionary if you need to.

As spring approaches, the days will begin to lengthen. Ancient people used to theorize that spring was a goddess who brought the growing season each year. They would celebrate each new season with dancing and feasting. These activities would testify to their belief in the goodness of creation. Events such as eclipses would frighten or even terrorize people, who believed that their bad behavior would irritate the gods. Thus they might glorify the gods in order to get a good crop. When that happened, it would strengthen their beliefs. Meanwhile, the monuments and other artifacts these people left behind still communicate to us today. Of course early people did not understand that spring comes because the earth revolves around the sun.

1. word: _____ meaning: _____

2. word: _____ meaning: _____

3. word: _____ meaning: _____

4. word: _____ meaning: _____

5. word: _____ meaning: _____

6. word: _____ meaning: _____

7. word: _____ meaning: _____

8. word: _____ meaning: _____

9. word: _____ meaning: _____

10. word: _____ meaning: _____

C. Vocabulary Challenge

Change each of the italicized words into a verb by using one of the suffixes in this lesson.

1. If you mark the ballot incorrectly, you will *invalid* your vote. _____

2. The heavy rains will *weak* the foundation. _____

3. I will not *dignity* that remark by replying. _____

4. Unfortunately, the effect of that TV show was to *trivial* a very important subject. _____

5. The lake will mostly *evaporation* during the hot summer. _____

Name _____ Date _____

Base Words and Suffixes

Teaching

A **suffix** is a word part added to the end of a base word. **Noun suffixes** are used to create nouns, usually from other parts of speech. Sometimes the spelling of the original word changes when you add the suffix.

exist + -ence ("state or quality of") = existence, "state or quality of existing"

The suffixes *–ance/-ence, -ation, -hood,* and *-cy* also mean "state or quality of."

Suffix	Example	Meaning
-ence, -ance	viol<u>ence</u>	state or quality of being violent
-ation	cultiv<u>ation</u>	state or quality of cultivating
-hood	adult<u>hood</u>	state or quality of being an adult
-cy	litera<u>cy</u>	state or quality of being literate

A. Suffixes in Action

Use one of the suffixes above to form a noun that will complete the second sentence of each pair. Form the noun from the italicized word in the first sentence.

1. Your statistics are always *accurate.* Your _____ rate is very high.

2. Do you *illustrate* your own books? This _____ is lovely.

3. "You must not *resist,*" said the alien warrior. _____ is futile."

4. She is a *widow* now. She has found that _____ is not easy at first.

5. We have *frequent* thunderstorms. In fact, their _____ is troublesome to my dog.

6. Do you *correspond* by e-mail? My _____ box is full right now.

7. Mr. Ramos is a new *father.* I think _____ suits him, don't you?

8. The child is *determined* to learn to crawl. Her _____ is inspiring.

9. Is he *absent* again? His _____ record is getting longer each week.

10. Who will *narrate* the play? The _____ is very important, you know.

Base Words and Suffixes

More Practice

B. Vocabulary in Action

In the passage below, circle ten words that end with the suffixes *-ance, -ence, -ation, -cy,* or *-hood.* Use your knowledge of word parts and context clues to predict what the words mean. Write the meaning of each example. Use a dictionary if you need to.

     Ever since childhood, Charles had an active imagination. Maybe it was even there in his infancy. Sometimes this quality seemed to get in the way of matters of importance in his life. His friends once formed a conspiracy to try to bring him out of his shell. But after awhile they realized that what might seem odd in other people was just normalcy for him, his way of striving for excellence. This quality of deep speculation was not a hindrance but rather a vital part of his very manhood.

1. word: _____ meaning: _____

2. word: _____ meaning: _____

3. word: _____ meaning: _____

4. word: _____ meaning: _____

5. word: _____ meaning: _____

6. word: _____ meaning: _____

7. word: _____ meaning: _____

8. word: _____ meaning: _____

9. word: _____ meaning: _____

10. word: _____ meaning: _____

C. Vocabulary Challenge

Change each of the following words into a noun, by using one of the suffixes in this lesson. Then write a sentence that uses the noun.

1. annoy _____

2. priest _____

3. utter _____

4. hesitant _____

5. appreciate _____

Anglo-Saxon Affixes and Base Words

Teaching

Lesson 12

Many words we use today come from the **Anglo-Saxon** language, an early form of English called Old English. **Affixes** are word parts that are added to the beginning (prefix) or the end (suffix) of **base words** or word parts to form new words. A base word is a complete word to which a prefix and/or a suffix may be added.

> base word meaning "a place where one lives, a residence"

> suffix from Old English meaning "in or toward a specified time, place, or direction"

home + ward = homeward

> word that means "toward or at home"

Examine the chart below.

Affix	Type	Meaning	Example
a-	prefix	on/in, in the act or direction of	*ahead*
be-	prefix	thoroughly, around, over; about; cause to become; to affect	*beloved*
for-	prefix	completely, excessively	*forsworn*
over-	prefix	above, excessive, superior	*overpass*
self-	prefix	oneself, automatic	*self-righteous*
-en	suffix	cause to be, to have, made of, resembling	*strengthen*
-like	suffix	resembling, characteristic of	*ladylike*
-some	suffix	characterized by a specified quality, group, or number	*troublesome*
-ward(s)	suffix	in or toward; specified direction	*downward*
-worthy	suffix	of sufficient worth; suitable or safe for	*seaworthy*

A. Anglo-Saxon Affixes and Base Words in Action

Add one of these affixes to the italicized word in each sentence to form a word that completes the sentence correctly.

a-	be-	for-	over-	self-
-en	-like	-some	-ward(s)	-worthy

1. Will you please *give* me for putting lizards in your hat? _____

2. Casey's *confidence* radiated but I knew he would strike out. _____

3. My dreams have given me a whole new level of *understanding*. _____

4. You can't *grudge* me one small piece of chocolate, Maya. _____

5. Ever since my brother lied, he's ceased to be *trust*. _____

6. The fuschia plane flew *up* into the blue haze. _____

7. The days *length* as we approach summer. _____

8. Oh, what a *bother* piece of mail! _____

9. You never cease to *maze* me, Matilda. _____

10. Her *violin* voice enchants me. _____

Anglo-Saxon Affixes and Base Words   *More Practice*

B. Vocabulary in Action

Use one of the words below to complete each sentence. Then use your
understanding of Anglo-Saxon affixes to write the definition of each word.

forlorn   bewitch   reddens   twosome   awash   weblike

1. The alley cat's green eyes _____ me.

   meaning: _____

2. Lucy has been _____ ever since her pet chameleon died.

   meaning: _____

3. My face _____ whenever you remind me of the time I ate slugs!

   meaning: _____

4. The sky is _____ with stars.

   meaning: _____

5. Mack and I have been a terrible _____ ever since we were five, so don't even try
   picking on us, Mister!

   meaning: _____

6. Amy fingered the _____ lace her grandmother had given her.

   meaning: _____

C. Vocabulary Challenge

For each base word, add an affix to form a new word. Use each word to
complete its matching sentence.

1. way _____

   The _____ travelers bathed their stinky feet in our drinking water.

2. _____ aggrandizing

   In his _____ way, he said he was a "scuba-diving, sky-diving, snowboarding, rocket
   scientist who saved fifteen maidens from a dragon"!

3. guile _____

   You _____ me with your beauty.

Name _____ Date _____

Roots and Word Families

A great many English words are put together from parts that come from other languages, such as Latin and Greek. These word parts are called **roots.** Roots cannot stand alone but must be combined with prefixes or suffixes to form words. A group of words with a common root is called a **word family.** You can often guess the meaning of a word by knowing the meaning of its root and its prefixes and suffixes.

Latin root	Meaning	Word family
aud	hear	audio, audition, audit
cred	trust or believe	creed, credible, credit
man	hand	manual, manage, maneuver
port	carry	porter, export, transport
spec	see	spectacle, inspect, suspect
voc	voice	vocal, invoke, vocation

The following tips can help you use roots to figure out the meaning of unfamiliar words such as *incredulous.*

   Break the word into its parts: (prefix) in- + (root) *cred* + (suffix) -ulous

Think of other words you know that have the root cred, such as *creed* and *credit.* Decide the meaning that they share—"believe" or "trust."

Think about the meaning of any prefixes or suffixes in the word: *in-* means "not" and *-ulous* means "full of" or "characterized by."

Put this information together to predict what *incredulous* means: "not being full of belief."

Check the context and a dictionary or glossary to see if your guess is correct. In this case, you will learn that *incredulous* means "skeptical; disbelieving" or "expressing disbelief."

A. Identifying Roots and Word Families

Underline the root of each word in Column A. Then match each word with its correct meaning in Column B. Write the letter of the correct meaning in the space provided. Use the chart to help you.

Column A

1. inaudible _____
2. spectator _____
3. manuscript _____
4. import _____
5. credo _____
6. advocate _____
7. manipulate _____
8. incredible _____
9. vociferous _____
10. manicure _____

Column B

A. something written by hand

B. a stated belief

C. to argue for a cause

D. a fingernail treatment

E. impossible to hear

F. unbelievable

G. one who observes

H. making a noisy outcry

I. to handle skillfully

J. to bring in

Roots and Word Families

More Practice

B. Roots and Word Families in Action

Predict the meaning of each underlined word following the tips on the previous page and using context clues given in the sentences.

1. At first nobody thought the earth revolves around the sun, but the idea gradually gained <u>credence</u> over time.

   meaning: _____

2. Alice realizes that she has a strong <u>vocation</u> for a religious career.

   meaning: _____

3. We'll be able to get our canoe down most of the river with no trouble, but we'll have to make a <u>portage</u> in one or two places where the water is low.

   meaning: _____

4. Juan's teacher told him he'd be good in the school play, so he's going to the <u>audition</u> today.

   meaning: _____

5. I've never seen such a <u>spectacular</u> fireworks display.

   meaning: _____

6. Put your latest drawings into your <u>portfolio</u> and bring them to school tomorrow.

   meaning: _____

C. Vocabulary Challenge

For each item, write the root shared by the two bold-faced words. Then write the meaning of the root, using your knowledge of roots and context clues. Check your answers in a dictionary.

1. Mr. Williams finds much wisdom in the **Scriptures.**

   Can you read the **inscription** on the tombstone?

   root: _____ meaning: _____

2. Please **dictate** your message to me.

   We are awaiting the jury's **verdict.**

   root: _____ meaning: _____

3. Reckless drivers act as if they were **immortal.**

   The funeral will be held at the **mortuary.**

   root: _____ meaning: _____

Name _____ Date _____

Roots and Word Families

A **root** is a word part that cannot stand alone. Many English words are based on roots that come from other languages, especially Latin and Greek. You can easily learn the meanings of some of these roots. Then, by recognizing prefixes and suffixes and looking for context clues, you'll find that you can understand many unfamiliar words. Note that words often belong to **word families** that share a common root.

Latin root	Meaning	Word family
doc	teach	doctrine, doctor, docile
ject	throw	reject, project, conjecture, jet
mem, ment	mind	memory, mental, mention
not	note or mark	note, notation, connote
sens, sent	feel	sense, sensation, consent
vert, ver	turn	reverse, vertical, versus

The following tips can help you use roots to figure out the meaning of unfamiliar words such as *insensate.*

Break the word into its parts: (prefix) in- + (root) *sens* + (suffix) -ate

Think of other words you know that have the root *sens*, such as *sense* and *sensation.* Decide the meaning that they share — "feeling" or "sensing."

Think about the meaning of any prefixes or suffixes in the word: *in-* means "not" and *-ate* means "characterized by."

Put this information together to predict what *insensate* means: "characterized by not feeling."

Check the context and a dictionary or glossary to see if your guess is correct. In this case, you will learn that *insensate* means "lacking sensation or awareness" or "unfeeling."

A. Identifying Roots and Word Families

Underline the root of each word in Column A. Then match each word with its correct meaning in Column B. Write the letter of the correct meaning in the space provided. Use the chart to help you.

Column A

1. documentary _____
2. projectile _____
3. denote _____
4. versatile _____
5. sentimental _____
6. indoctrinate _____
7. introverted _____
8. eject _____
9. dissent _____
10. demented _____

Column B

A. to throw out forcibly; expel

B. mentally ill; insane

C. turned inward

D. showing factual material

E. to mark; indicate

F. able to turn to different things

G. to differ in opinion or feeling

H. an object thrown or fired

I. swayed by emotion more than reason

J. to instruct in a point of view

Roots and Word Families *More Practice*

B. Roots and Word Families in Action

Predict the meaning of each underlined word following the tips on the previous page and using context clues given in the sentences.

1. If too much of the rain forest is destroyed, the damage will be <u>irreversible</u>.

   meaning: _____

2. You should pay attention not only to the literal meanings of words—their denotations—but also to their <u>connotations</u>.

   meaning: _____

3. The two girls have much in common, but there are some <u>notable</u> differences between them.

   meaning: _____

4. Her sister is a quiet person and a loner, but Janet is a real <u>extrovert</u>.

   meaning: _____

5. A springtime garden is full of <u>sensuous</u> delights.

   meaning: _____

6. I really don't know how our team is going to do this year. All I can offer is a <u>conjecture</u>.

   meaning: _____

C. Vocabulary Challenge

For each item, write the root shared by the two bold-faced words. Then write the meaning of the root, using your knowledge of roots and context clues. Check your answers in a dictionary.

1. The **population** has increased since the last census.
   Hip-hop is **popular** these days.

   root: _____ meaning: _____

2. My dad has a new **tractor.**
   I've always been **attracted** to science fiction.

   root: _____ meaning: _____

3. Nobody ever thought of that idea before; it's really quite **novel.**
   This year's model has some **innovations** that really improve its performance.

   root: _____ meaning: _____

Name _____   Date _____

Roots and Word Families

Teaching

A **word family** is a group of words that share the same root. Roots have come into
the English language from other languages such as Latin and Greek. A **root** cannot
stand alone, but it carries its meaning into an English word when it is combined with
one or more prefixes, suffixes, or other roots. Knowing the meanings of some of these
roots and other word parts can help you figure out the meaning of an unfamiliar word.

Greek root/Combining form	Meaning	Word family
chron	time	chronic, synchronize, chronometer
gen	race, family	genesis, genre, genius
gram	something written	telegram, diagram, grammar
log	word	dialogue, logic, apology
phon	sound	telephone, phonograph, phonetic

The following tips can help you use roots to figure out the meaning of unfamiliar
words such as *synchronize.*

Break the word into its parts: (prefix) syn- + (root) *chron* + (suffix) -ize.

Think of other words you know that have the same root, such as chronological.
Decide the meaning that they share—"time."

Think about the meaning of any prefixes or suffixes in the word: syn- means
"together" or "with," and -ize means "to cause to be or to become."

Put this information together to predict what *synchronize* means: "to cause to be
together in time."

Check the context and a dictionary or glossary to see if your guess is correct. In this
case, you will learn that *synchronize* means "to cause to occur at the same time"
or "to be simultaneous."

A. Identifying Roots and Word Families

Underline the root of each word in Column A. Then match each word with its
correct meaning in Column B. Write the letter of the correct meaning in the space
provided. Use the chart to help you.

Column A

1. monophonic _____
2. chronicle _____
3. genealogy _____
4. monogram _____
5. megaphone _____
6. chronometer _____
7. phonetics _____
8. genocide _____
9. monologue _____
10. ideology _____

Column B

A. device that measures time precisely

B. set of ideas, doctrines, or beliefs

C. study of speech sounds

D. extermination of an entire people

E. having a single melody or tune

F. long speech by one person

G. study of ancestry; family tree

H. device to amplify the voice

I. record of events happening over time

J. design of one or more initials

Roots and Word Families

More Practice

B. Roots and Word Families in Action

Predict the meaning of each underlined word following the tips on the previous page and using context clues given in the sentences. Use a dictionary to check your answers.

1. The old man gazed fondly at his <u>progeny</u>, all the way down to his great-grandchildren, who had come to celebrate his birthday.

   meaning: _____

2. You can use wind power to <u>generate</u> electricity.

   meaning: _____

3. When he had something to say he could say it neatly and cleverly in one brief, witty <u>epigram</u>.

   meaning: _____

4. At the senator's funeral, the governor, who had known him well, delivered a very moving <u>eulogy</u>.

   meaning: _____

5. Is that pain in your knee <u>chronic</u>, or are you just having it today?

   meaning: _____

6. I didn't read the whole book. In fact, I never got beyond the <u>prologue</u>.

   meaning: _____

C. Vocabulary Challenge

For each item, write the Greek root shared by the two bold-faced words. Then write the meaning of the root, using your knowledge of roots and context clues. Check your answers in a dictionary.

1. They've built a **hydroelectric** plant by the river.

   Could I have a drink of water? I'm **dehydrated** from all that exercise.

   root: _____ meaning: _____

2. He's a real **misanthrope** and has no use for humanity.

   I plan to study **anthropology.**

   root: _____ meaning: _____

3. I really don't know that writer's name; she goes by a **pseudonym.**

   Astronomers tend to regard astrology as a **pseudoscience.**

   root: _____ meaning: _____

Lesson 16 Middle English Words   *Teaching*

In 1066, an important historical event—the Norman Conquest—forever altered the English language. England was now ruled by the Normans, who lived in what was later to become France. New words began flooding into English from other languages, especially French and Latin. By 1150, Old English had become **Middle English.** In a dictionary you can trace a word's history, or **etymology,** from its earliest roots.

> **mansion** [Middle English, a dwelling, from Old French, from Latin *manere*, to dwell, remain]

The etymology of *mansion* tells you that it came into English from the Middle English period (1150-1500 A.D.), where it meant "a dwelling," and was taken from Old French, which in turn took it from the Latin word *manere*, which means "to dwell," or "to remain."

English Words Taken from Middle English

attorney	soldier	lantern	beef	captain
gown	jury	serpent	language	orange
merchandise	court	liberty	spy	pigeon
melody	money	nature	porpoise	ambush

A. Identifying Middle English Words

From the word bank above, choose the word that matches each of the following etymologies.

1. (ME, Old French *jure*, Anglo Norman *jurer*, "to swear") _____

2. (ME *soudier*, "mercenary," Old French *soudoior*, Latin *solidum*, "pay") _____

3. (ME *melodie*, Old French, Late Latin *melodia*, Greek *meloidia*, "singing") _____

4. (ME, Old French *buef*, Latin bos, bov, "cow") _____

5. (ME, Old French *pume orenge*, Old Italian *melarancio*, earlier from Arabic, from Sanskrit, "fruit of

   the orange tree" _____

6. (ME, "essential properties of a thing," Old French, Latin *natura*, from *nasci*, "to be born")

   _____

7. (ME *capitain*, Old French, Late Latin *capitaneus*, Latin *caput*, "head") _____

8. (ME *liberte*, Old French, Latin *libertas*, from *liber*, "free" _____

9. (ME, Old French *pijon*, Late Latin *pipio*, "young chirping bird," from *pipire*, "to chirp"

   _____

10. (ME *embush*, Old French *embuschier*, from Frankish *buscu*, "woods, bush" _____

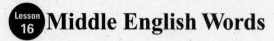

Lesson 16 **Middle English Words**   *More Practice*

B. Vocabulary Words in Action

Choose the correct word from the word bank on the previous page to complete each sentence. Use the short etymology of each word to help you.

1. Jenny wore a silver (ME goune, Old French/Late Latin *gunna,* "leather garment) to the St.

   Valentine's Day ball. _____

2. Do we have enough (ME, Latin *moneta,* "mint, coinage") to eat dinner at that new restaurant?

   _____

3. We used a kerosene (ME, Greek *lampein,* "to shine") when the power went out. _____

4. The documentary focused on a deadly Australian (ME, Latin *serpere,* "to creep"). _____

5. If you sue the company, you will have to hire an (ME, Old French *atorner,* "to appoint").

   _____

6. Mari wants to learn Spanish so she can speak another (ME, Latin *lingua,* "tongue"). _____

7. A (ME, Old French *porc peis,* "pig fish") leaped out of the water near our sailboat. _____

8. The (ME, Old French *espier,* "to watch") collected information about the regime for the opposition.

   _____

9. All the (ME, Old French *marchandise,* "trade") in that store is on sale. _____

10. The district attorney will meet us in (ME, Latin *cohors,* "courtyard"). _____

C. Vocabulary Challenge

Look up the etymologies of these words in a dictionary and write them in the blanks.

1. slander _____

   _____

2. lavish _____

   _____

3. humble _____

   _____

4. courage _____

   _____

5. legend _____

   _____

Lesson 17 # Modern English

Modern English is full of words from other languages. Many have been taken from languages such as French, Spanish, and Italian. Many more come from the German, Japanese, Chinese, Arabic, and South Pacific languages.

The *commandant* of the prisoner-of-war camp was very strict.

The word *commandant* comes from the French language, and is a form of the word *comander,* meaning "to command." The definition is "the commanding officer of a military organization." You might think the word would be pronounced **k man dant,** like the word *command.* However, in French the pronunciation is **kom n dant,** and the pronunciation stayed with the word when it was taken into English.

French		Spanish	Italian	Japanese
antique	charade	guava	concerto	judo
ballet	bureau	fiesta	graffiti	haiku
beret	mirage	guacamole	cello	kimono
boutique	morale	macho	spaghetti	sushi
debut	plateau	poncho	studio	samurai
chaperone	sabotage	siesta	extravaganza	karaoke

A. Foreign Words in Action

For each word below, write another word from the chart that has a similar pronunciation pattern. Then circle the correct phonetic respelling. Use a dictionary to help you.

1. BALLET (bă-lā') or (băl'ət) Word: _____

2. TOFU (tō'fyoo) or (tō'foo) Word: _____

3. ANTIQUE (ān-tēk') or (ăn-tik') Word: _____

4. CHARADE (shə-rād') or (shī'rād) Word: _____

5. PLATEAU (plă-too') or (plă-tō') Word: _____

6. SABOTAGE (săb'ə-täzh') or (săb'ə-tach') Word: _____

7. SIESTA (sē-ĕs'tə) or (si-ĕs'tə) Word: _____

8. GUACAMOLE (gä-kə-mo'lē) or (gwä-kə-mō'lē) Word: _____

9. SPAGHETTI (spə-gĕt'ē) or (spə-gēt-ī) Word: _____

10. CONCERTO (kən-ser'tō) or (kən-chĕr'to) Word: _____

Modern English   *More Practice*

B. Vocabulary in Action

The brief etymologies below leave out the language information. Match each etymology to a word from the chart. Write the word in the blank, followed by the name of the language from which it came into Modern English.

1. from *saboter,* "to walk noisily," from sabot, "old shoe" _____

2. from *graffio,* "a scratch or scribble" _____

3. from *kara,* "empty," + oke, "orchestra" _____

4. from *mirer,* "to look at," from mirus, "wonderful" _____

5. "warrior," from *samurafi,* sa (meaning unknown) + morafi,

   "to watch," mor, "to guard" _____

6. from *platel,* "platter," from plat, "flat" _____

7. from *berret,* "cap" _____

8. from *sexta* (hora), "sixth (hour)", "midday" _____

9. from *antiquus,* "old" _____

10. from *festa,* "feast" _____

C. Vocabulary Challenge

Write two words from the chart to complete each sentence in a way that makes sense. Use two words that share a pronunciation pattern.

1. The dancer wears a _____ in the new _____.

2. That _____ sells both clothing and an occasional _____.

3. Do you prefer eating the fruit of the _____ tree or _____ dip?

4. He thinks he looks pretty _____ in that _____.

5. The artist creates unusual _____ using his mama's _____.

Analyzing Roots, Base Words, and Affixes

Teaching

Base words are words that can stand alone. Other words are made up of base words or **roots** (word parts that cannot stand alone) and **affixes** (prefixes and suffixes). Breaking a difficult word into smaller parts can help you understand its meaning.

prefix that means "below, beneath, or under" or "too little"

hypo- + *derm* + -ic = hypodermic

root that means "skin"   adjective suffix that means "relating to"   word that means "under the skin"

Base words sometimes change spelling when combined with other word parts. If you are unsure of the spelling of a word, check a dictionary.

This chart shows some common Greek roots, also called **combining forms.**

Greek roots/combining forms

arch or *archi* (rule, govern, or chief)	*hypo* (below, beneath, under, or too little)
auto (self)	*meter* or *metr* (measure)
chron (time)	*mono* (one or single)
crat or *cracy* (rule or government)	*lith* (stone)
dem (people)	*log* (idea, word, or study)
derm (skin)	*plut* (wealth)
haem or *hem* (blood)	*techn* (art or skill)
hydr (water)	*therm* (heat)
hyper (above or too much)	

A. Identifying Greek Roots, Base Words, and Affixes

For each item, write the letter of the correct meaning in the blank. Use the chart above and your knowledge of word parts to help you. You may also use a dictionary if needed.

1. monoplane _____

2. chronometer _____

3. architect _____

4. meritocracy _____

5. monorail _____

6. dermatologist _____

7. chronic _____

8. chronological _____

9. plutocratic _____

10. hyperthermia _____

A. a doctor who treats skin diseases

B. an airplane with one set of wings

C. arranged in order of occurrence

D. a railway system that uses a single rail

E. continuing; long-lasting

F. a device that takes precise measurements of time

G. government by the most qualified people

H. governed by the rich

I. a person who designs buildings

J. extremely high body temperature

Analyzing Roots, Base Words, and Affixes

More Practice

B. Greek Roots, Base Words, and Affixes in Action

For each item, circle the word that fits the sentence. Use the chart on the previous page, context clues, and your knowledge of word parts to help you. You may also use a dictionary if needed.

1. Shana delivered quite a (monologue, dialogue); she spoke for 20 minutes and didn't let me say a word!

2. The general wanted the new government to be an (autocracy, architect) in which he had all the power.

3. An airplane that is on (autopilot, biplane) flies a preset course with little or no help from the people on the plane.

4. We saw a science fiction movie about (plutospace, hyperspace), a universe where space has more than three dimensions.

5. Our teacher reminded us to use the (democratic, metric) system when taking measurements for our science projects.

6. You are sure to become (dehydrated, chronic) if you stay out in the sun without drinking any fluids.

7. Ali read a comic book about a superhero and the evil genius who is her (archenemy, technician).

8. The (technocrat, monolith) was made of a single huge chunk of granite.

9. Firefighters use (hydrants, rehydrators) to tap into a city or town's water system.

10. A (hypertext, autotext) document contains links to the World Wide Web or other electronic documents and can be read in more ways than a traditional book.

C. Vocabulary Challenge

For each item, circle the word or phrase that answers each question. Use a dictionary if needed.

1. Is **hematology** the study of skin or the study of blood?

2. Is a **hyperactive** child energetic or lazy?

3. Is a **prologue** a speech that comes before the play or after the play?

4. Is an account of historical events an **autograph** or a **chronicle**?

5. Is a **monotone** a way of speaking or a way of traveling?

Lesson 19 # Analyzing Roots and Affixes   *Teaching*

Analyzing word parts is a good way to get an idea of a word's meaning. These word parts include **roots,** which are word parts that cannot stand alone; and **affixes,** which are word parts added to the beginning (prefix) or end (suffix) of base words and roots to form new words.

(prefix that means "within")   (root that means "look at" or "see")

intro- + *spect* + **-ive** = **introspective**

(suffix that means "relating to")   (word that means "looking within" or "examining one's own feelings and thoughts")

Base words sometimes change spelling when combined with other word parts. If you are unsure of the spelling of a word, check a dictionary.

Study the common Latin roots and affixes in the charts below.

Prefix	Latin Root	Suffix
de- (not)	*cess* (go)	-ary (relating to)
pro- (forward)	*duct* (lead)	-ation, -ion, -sion (state or quality of)
re- (again *or* back)	*ject* (throw)	-d/ed (changes verb tense from present to past)
trans- (across)	*pel* or *pul* (drive or thrust)	-er, -or (one who is or does)
in- *or* im- (in *or* within)	*port* (carry)	-ful (full of)
intra- *or* intro- (within)	*spect* (look)	-ing (indicates ongoing action)
con- (with)	*tempor* (time)	-ive (relating to)
	tract (pull)	-s, -es (makes a noun plural or a verb present tense)

A. Identifying Roots and Affixes

For each item, write the letter of the correct meaning in the blank. Use the chart above and your knowledge of word parts to help you. You may also use a dictionary if needed.

1. reject _____
2. conductor _____
3. inspection _____
4. detracts _____
5. repelled _____
6. transporting _____
7. procession _____
8. respectful _____
9. prospective _____
10. propulsion _____

A. a group moving forward in an orderly manner

B. someone who leads an orchestra

C. likely to happen in the future

D. takes away; diminishes

E. the act of pushing forward, often by mechanical means

F. refuse or throw back

G. bringing or carrying

H. full of high regard; polite

I. a careful look at something

J. driven back or pushed away

Lesson 19 — Analyzing Roots and Affixes

More Practice

B. Roots and Affixes in Action

For each item, circle the word that fits the sentence. Use the chart on the previous page, context clues, and your knowledge of word parts to help you. You may also use a dictionary if needed.

1. A (reporter, reductive) gathers news for a newspaper, magazine, radio station, TV show, or Web site.

2. My favorite singer was recently (inducted, detracted) into the Rock and Roll Hall of Fame.

3. This movie (respects, repulses) me—it's disgusting. Turn it off!

4. (Introductions, Contractions) have fewer letters than the words they replace. For example, *don't* is a contraction of *do not*.

5. Marta asked if I would need (transportation, transduction) to her house, but I told her that my older brother would give me a ride.

6. You seem awfully (injected, dejected). What's bothering you?

7. A movie (protractor, projector) throws an image onto a large screen.

8. "This class is just a(n) (propulsion, introduction) to the subject of American history," our teacher said. "You will learn much more about it in future classes."

9. Nancy and Frieda had a long, drawn-out, (recessed, protracted) argument about which of them is a better basketball player.

10. Leonardo da Vinci was a (contemporary, transporter) of Michelangelo; in other words, both artists lived at the same time.

C. Vocabulary Challenge

For each item below, form two words using the affixes. Then write the new word that best completes each sentence. Use context clues, the chart on the previous page, and your knowledge of word parts to help you. You may also use a dictionary if needed.

1. (*de-*, *pro-*) motion

   My father was excited about his

   _____.

   Ms. Beck's _____ from vice president to assistant was a shock.

2. (*dis-*, *re-*) cover

   The doctor says Sonia will soon

   _____ from her fall.

   The expedition hopes to _____ a new species of dinosaur.

3. thank (*-ful*, *-less*)

   Cleaning the birdcage was a

   _____ task, let me tell you.

   The lost climbers were _____ to be rescued at last.

4. research (*-er*, *-ing*)

   The _____ worked on her experiments, taking notes all the while.

   Shaleena and Marcy are _____ the history of women's rights.

Analyzing Roots and Affixes

Lesson 20

Teaching

If you see a word that you do not recognize, analyze its parts to get an idea of its meaning. Many words can be broken into **roots,** which are word parts that cannot stand alone, and **affixes,** which are word parts added to the beginning (prefix) or end (suffix) of base words and roots to form new words.

(prefix that means "under, below, or beneath") (suffix that means "state or quality of")

sub- + *ordin* + -ate = subordinate

(root that means "order, rank, or series") (word that means "lower in order or rank")

Study the common roots and affixes in the charts below.

Prefix	Latin Root	Suffix
circum- (around)	*cept* (take)	*-able* or *-ible* (able to be)
in- (not)	*equ* or *equi* (equal)	*-ance* (state or quality of)
inter- (among or between)	*ject* (throw)	*-ation, -ion, -sion* (state or quality of)
per- (through, very, or intensely)	*miss* or *mit* (send *or* let go)	*-d, ed* (changes verb tense from
pre- (before)	*ord* or *ordin* (order, rank,	present to past)
re- (again or back)	or series)	*-ive* (likely to)
sub- (under, below, or beneath)	*spect* (look)	
	ven or *vent* (come)	
	vert or *vers* (turn)	

A. Identifying Roots and Affixes

For each item, write the letter of the correct meaning in the blank. Use the chart above and your knowledge of word parts to help you. You may also use a dictionary if needed.

1. prevent _____

2. reversed _____

3. equitable _____

4. permissive _____

5. circumvent _____

6. interception _____

7. perspective _____

8. interject _____

9. ordinance _____

10. intermission _____

A. stopping or interrupting the progress of something

B. fair, just

C. put between or among other things

D. a command, order, or law

E. keep something from happening

F. go around

G. a way of seeing things

H. turned around

I. a break between acts of a play

J. not strict

Lesson 20 **Analyzing Roots and Affixes**   *More Practice*

B. Roots and Affixes in Action

For each item, circle the word that fits the sentence. Use the chart on the previous page, context clues, and your knowledge of word parts to help you. You may also use a dictionary if needed.

1. Please (precept, remit) your payment of $16 within 10 days.

2. David was (circumspect, intercepted) while walking through the dark parking lot; he looked around him often and listened for strange noises.

3. It was very (submissive, perceptive) of you to know what Raquel wanted for her birthday without even asking her.

4. The soldier was punished for (permission, insubordination), or failure to obey orders.

5. My favorite comic book is about a superhero who does everything he can to (subvert, interject) the plans of evildoers.

6. Dr. Rothschiller specializes in (preventive, reversion) medicine; she wants to change people's diet and exercise patterns before they get sick.

7. "Your (intervention, respect) kept me from making a mistake," Dan said. "I'm glad you stepped in."

8. Eleanor was (inequable, receptive) to our plan. "What a great idea!" she said.

9. Our teacher (intercepted, ordination) the note we were passing around, and I don't know if he will give it back to us.

10. Is it (permissible, reversible) to chew gum in class, or will we be punished for it?

C. Vocabulary Challenge

The word bank below is made up of words with Latin roots. For each item, choose the appropriate word and write it in the blank. Use context clues and your knowledge of word parts to help you. You may also use a dictionary if needed.

sens (feel): insensitive, sensation

cogn (know): recognize, cognitive

init (beginning): initial

1. The feeling of an ice cube being put down the back of your shirt is an unpleasant

   _____.

2. I don't _____ that person. Is she someone we know?

3. That was an _____ remark. I think you hurt his feelings!

4. My _____ plan didn't work, so I have made many changes to it since.

5. English class helps students develop _____, or thinking, skills.

Name _____ Date _____

Specialized Vocabulary

Teaching

People in different jobs and areas of study often use a **specialized vocabulary.**
In many cases you can use context clues—examples, restatement, and definition—
to figure out the meaning of a specialized word. In the following sentences the
context clues for each italicized word are shown in boldface type.

Examples	Our *horticulture* class taught us skills, such as **how to grow fruits and vegetables, how to start seedlings, and how to prune older plants.**
Definition	First we learned to *fertilize*—**to spread compost on the soil to make it suitable for growing.**
Restatement	The *naturalist,* **a woman who is an expert in plants and wildflowers, brought in examples from her own garden.**

Example clues are often signaled by the phrases *that is, for example,* or *such as.*
Definitions and restatements may be set off by dashes or commas.

A. Specialized Vocabulary in Action

Underline the words or phrases that provide clues to the meaning of each word in italics.
Use the words you have underlined to help you write a definition for each specialized word.

1. We've been *cultivating,* that is, planting vegetables and flowers, on this vacant lot for many years.

   meaning: _____

2. The new *greenhouse,* a glassed-in structure for growing plants in all seasons, will be built on this site.

   meaning: _____

3. We haven't enough space to grow *cereal* crops such as wheat and corn.

   meaning: _____

4. We have planted patches of *legumes,* which are peas, beans, and related vegetables.

   meaning: _____

5. We plant many varieties because a *monoculture*—an area planted with a single vegetable or flower—is bad for the soil.

   meaning: _____

6. We were shown how *hybrids,* which are grown by combining two different varieties of a plant, can produce unique flowers or healthier fruit.

   meaning: _____

7. We all take turns *deadheading,* that is, cutting or pinching off dead flowers as they fade to encourage new flowering growth.

   meaning: _____

8. Some of us have *herbariums,* which are collections of dried leaves and flowers mounted on paper.

   meaning: _____

Specialized Vocabulary

B. Vocabulary Words in Action

Underline eight examples of definition, restatement, or example clues in the passage below. Then use each example to infer or predict the meaning of each italicized (specialized) word.

Our community used a vacant lot to plant several beds, or small garden areas, of flowers. We planted many *species* of wildflower, such as coneflowers, sunflowers, and buttercups. We also *transplanted* some of our indoor flowers; in other words, we moved them from pots to the garden soil. Other people brought *seedlings*—small plants just beginning to grow—to add to the mix. Some people like *formal gardens,* which are gardens laid out in regular patterns. But we *sow,* or plant, our seeds and flowers any old place. An adult friend brings us *organic matter,* including animal waste and plant material, to use as fertilizer. We add this to the *topsoil*—the soil at the surface of the ground.

1. beds meaning: _____

2. species meaning: _____

3. transplanted meaning: _____

4. seedlings meaning: _____

5. formal gardens meaning: _____

6. sow meaning: _____

7. organic matter meaning: _____

8. topsoil meaning: _____

C. Vocabulary Challenge

Circle the specialized word in each sentence below. Then underline the definition, restatement, or example clue. Finally, use the clue to determine the meaning of the specialized word.

1. Many people plant gardens to attract bluebirds, woodpeckers, and other ornithological species.

   meaning: _____

2. Berry trees and blocks of suet—fatty material that provides energy—will bring many birds to a yard.

   meaning: _____

3. Planting native species, the types of plants found originally in an area, will bring native birds.

   meaning: _____

4. Butterflies flock to a yard where they can feed on nectar, which is the sugary juice of flowers.

   meaning: _____

Specialized Vocabulary

Teaching

You have learned that people who work in specialized areas, such as computers or medicine, often use **specialized vocabularies.** You are probably already familiar with many of these words. When you come across one you don't know, look for examples, definitions, and restatements to help you understand them. In the following sentences, context clues for the words in italics are shown in boldface type.

Definition   Jed played *shortstop,* **which is the position between second base and third base,** in the championship game.

Restatement   The Tigers, Eagles, and Ravens all play in the same *league,* or **group of teams.**

Example   One team kept making *errors,* **from dropped balls to overthrows to bad plays.**

Remember to look for signal words and phrases—*such as, that is, for example*— that will indicate context clues. Also pay attention to dashes and commas, which may also set off helpful words.

A. Specialized Vocabulary in Action

Underline the words or phrases that provide clues to the meaning of each word in italics. Use the words you have underlined to help you write a definition for the meaning of each specialized word.

1. The *spectators*—parents, friends, and enthusiastic fans—yelled themselves hoarse.

   meaning: _____

2. In a notebook I kept the team *statistics,* the totals of hits, runs, and errors for all the players.

   meaning: _____

3. The batter hit a *ground ball* that rolled straight through the infield.

   meaning: _____

4. The batter hit a *foul ball* but was called out when the opposing first-basemen caught the ball.

   meaning: _____

5. We hoped to attend the whole *series*—all four games between our team and the Falcons.

   meaning: _____

6. After trailing 4-2 for three innings, the Eagles suddenly scored five runs in a stunning *comeback.*

   meaning: _____

7. The next player hit a *double*—a two-base hit—and brought home the tying run from third.

   meaning: _____

8. In the ninth inning the batter *bunted*—hit the ball lightly—so the pitcher had to run in to scoop it up.

   meaning: _____

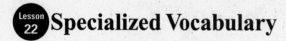

Specialized Vocabulary

Lesson 22

B. Vocabulary in Action

Underline ten examples of definition, restatement, or example clues in the passage below. Then use each example to determine or predict the meaning of each italicized word.

My sister wins a lot of *swim meets,* or competitions. She does well using a variety of different *strokes,* such as the crawl, the freestyle, and the backstroke. My brother is a tennis whiz and his dream is to play in a *Grand Slam* tournament, one of the top four tennis tournaments in the world. My mom does well with any game using a *cue stick,* such as pool or billiards. Dad likes to *crew;* that is, he works on a boat for friends who have sailboats. He meets them at the local *marina,* or docking area. Nothing makes him happier than puttering around on sailboats, *schooners,* and other small boats. My sport is wrestling. I have *pinned* many opponents, which means I have held both their shoulders to the floor until the *referee,* or official judge, awards me points. I've always liked *contact sports,* such as wrestling, hockey, or football.

1. meets meaning: _____

2. strokes meaning: _____

3. Grand Slam meaning: _____

4. cue stick meaning: _____

5. crew meaning: _____

6. marina meaning: _____

7. schooner meaning _____

8. pinned meaning: _____

9. referee meaning: _____

10. contact sport meaning: _____

C. Vocabulary Challenge

Find and circle the specialized word in each sentence below. Then underline the definition, restatement, or example clue. Finally, use the clue to determine the meaning of the specialized word.

1. The placekicker whose job is to make the point after touchdown came out on the field.

   meaning: _____

2. The cheerleaders completed a basket toss, hurling one high into the air and then catching her in their arms.

   meaning: _____

3. Favorite women's gymnastic events include floor exercise, uneven parallel bars, and balance beam.

   meaning: _____

Specialized Words

Lesson 23

As you know, people with different occupations or specialties use **specialized vocabulary.** Remember that to determine the meaning of an unfamiliar vocabulary word, you can use context clues—definition, restatement, and example. In the following sentences, context clues for the words in italics are shown in boldface type.

Definition	Our plane had *tandem* seating, **which means the seats were placed one behind the other.**
Restatement	The pilot *banked,* or **tilted the aircraft to one side,** so we could see the waterfall.
Example	We studied the elements of *aviation,* **such as construction, flying, and maintenance of aircraft.**

A. Specialized Vocabulary in Action

Underline the words or phrases that provide clues to the meaning of each word in italics. Use the words you have underlined to help you write a definition of each specialized word.

1. Once the plane took off, the stunt pilot performed a series of *acrobatics,* such as banks, dives, and wing-walking.

   meaning: _____

2. At a certain *altitude,* or the distance above the earth, pilots may lose consciousness.

   meaning: _____

3. While passengers boarded the hot-air balloon, it was *tethered,* or tied, to the ground.

   meaning: _____

4. The plane was loaded with such *cargo* as mail, food supplies, and medicines, for the flight to the disaster zone.

   meaning: _____

5. We flew in a *glider*—an aircraft without an engine that moves on the air currents—with our father.

   meaning: _____

6. Charles Lindbergh flew by *dead reckoning*—using calculated guesswork to navigate.

   meaning: _____

7. The plane taxied to the *hangar,* a large building where airplanes are serviced and housed.

   meaning: _____

8. The pilot pulled back on the *throttle;* the lever that regulates the airplane's speed.

   meaning: _____

Lesson 23 **Specialized Words**

B. Vocabulary Words in Action

Underline ten examples of definition, restatement or example clues and. Use each example to determine the meaning of each italicized word.

     The history of aviation includes stories about *aviators,* the people who pilot planes. The Wright Brothers, who made the first U.S. flight in 1903, built and flew a *biplane,* which is a two-winged plane. In 1909 a French inventor flew a *monoplane*—a single-winged plane—across the English Channel. Many early plane designs had no *navigation* equipment; that is, pilots could not plot and follow a course correctly. Such planes were often used by pilots who went *barnstorming,* performing acrobatics, wing-walking, and other stunts. A safer plane called the *trimotor*—with three engines—was developed in Germany in the early 20's. In 1927 Charles Lindbergh made the first *solo* flight across the Atlantic; that is, he flew the entire distance by himself. As planes began to fly higher, *pressurized cabins*—passenger areas with normal air pressure—became necessary. *Gyropilots,* which allowed a plane to fly automatically, came into use during the 1930's. Planes also became more *streamlined,* which means they were designed to offer less wind resistance and fly faster.

1. aviators meaning: _____

2. biplane meaning: _____

3. monoplane meaning: _____

4. navigation meaning: _____

5. barnstorming meaning: _____

6. trimotor meaning: _____

7. solo meaning: _____

8. pressurized cabins meaning: _____

9. gyropilots meaning: _____

10. streamlined meaning: _____

C. Vocabulary Challenge

Circle the specialized word in each sentence and underline the definition, restatement, or example clue. Write the meaning of the specialized word.

1. The pilot's tachometer—an instrument that measures speed—told her the speed had dropped.

    meaning: _____

2. The plane stalled; that is, its low speed caused the engine to stop.

    meaning: _____

3. The pilot ejected and pulled the cord on her parachute, which allowed her to float safely to earth.

    meaning: _____

Words with Multiple Meanings

Lesson 24

Many English words have more than one meaning. A **pitcher** on the baseball field is different from a **pitcher** full of juice on the table, even though both words are spelled and pronounced the same. Look at the dictionary entry below.

> **tack•le** (tăk′əl) *n.* The equipment used in a particular activity, especially in fishing; gear. The act of stopping an opposing player carrying the ball, especially by fording the opposition to the ground, as in football or Rugby. Either of the two line players on a team positioned between the guard and the end. *v.* To grab hold of and wrestle with (an opponent). To stop (an opponent carrying the ball), especially by forcing the opponent to the ground. To engage or deal with: *tackle a perplexing problem.*

Read these two sentences. Which meaning of the word **tackle** is used in each one?

Look in my **tackle** box for an extra hook.

The runner was brought down by Jed's last-minute **tackle**.

A. Multiple Meaning in Action

Two familiar words—**block** and **fall**—appear below with several of their meanings. For each sentence that follows the definitions, choose the letter of the meaning that best fits the word in italics.

block
A. (noun) one in a set of wooden or plastic toys
B. (noun) a rectangular section of a city or town
C. (verb) to shut out from view
D. (verb) in sports, the act of stopping an opposing player or ball
E. (verb) to stop the passage or movement of something or someone

fall
F. (verb) to drop from a higher place
G. (verb) to drop wounded or dead
H. (noun) a dropping from a higher place
I. (noun) autumn
J. (noun) artificial hair attached to regular hair

_____ 1. My sister likes to jog around the *block* after dinner.

_____ 3. Ten senators *blocked* the passage of the bill.

_____ 5. Sit down, or you'll *block* my view of the stage.

_____ 7. The infant built a tower of *blocks,* then knocked it down.

_____ 9. "*Block* that kick!" yelled the fans.

_____ 2. Many soldiers will *fall* in today's battle.

_____ 4. I like *fall,* with its brisk winds and colorful trees.

_____ 6. Geena wore a long braided *fall* with her new outfit.

_____ 8. Snowboarders often *fall* on that difficult ski run.

_____ 10. Jose took a painful *fall* from his skateboard.

Lesson 24

Words with Multiple Meanings

B. Vocabulary Words in Action

Read the different definitions for each word. Then complete each sentence by writing the correct word. In the blank after each sentence, write the letter of the word's correct meaning.

march

A. (verb) to walk in step with others

B. (noun) a form of music

C. (noun) a long, tiring journey on foot

bridge

D. (noun) a structure over a river or road

E. (noun) the upper, bony part of the nose

F. (noun) an arrangement of false teeth

1. My glasses kept slipping down the _____ of my nose. _____

2. The band started the concert with a brisk _____. _____

3. The soldiers were exhausted after their _____. _____

4. The accident knocked Mr. Lewis's _____ from his mouth. _____

5. The marathon runners took an hour to cross the _____. _____

C. Vocabulary Challenge

Choose the word from each set of four that makes sense in both sentences that follow. Use a dictionary if you need help.

1. *hunt, flower, hide, plant*

   Karen will _____ the clues for the treasure hunt.

   I found a _____ in my yard I have never seen before.

2. *pan, move, shoot, piece*

   Watch the camera _____ across the faces of the astronauts.

   Set the _____ of cake on the counter.

Lesson 25

Synonyms

Teaching

Synonyms are words that have the same or almost the same meaning. However, these small differences can determine which one you should use in a sentence.

Look at the thesaurus entry below for the word *hesitate*.

> **hesitate:** *verb;* Synonyms: *waver, falter, stammer, stumble, pause*

When asked to risk his life, the courageous warrior did not *waver*.

When asked to risk his life, the courageous warrior did not *stumble*.

The words *waver* and *stumble* are synonyms. Yet although they have similar meanings, they are not identical. In the first sentence above, to not *waver* suggests not losing confidence, while in the second sentence to not *stumble* suggests not falling or tripping physically. This makes *waver* the best choice for this sentence.

A. Synonyms in Action

Read each of the following sentences. Underline the word in parentheses that best completes the sentence and use a dictionary or thesaurus if needed.

1. The gang (stole, captured, abducted) the ambassador and took him to their hideout.

2. The beaten man could not identify his (assailant, foe, criminal) to the police.

3. After several accidents, Carl had his driving license (cancelled, revoked, removed).

4. The (assassin, killer, attacker) agreed to take part in the plot against the prime minister.

5. The (throng, crowd, mob) of people at the concert was so thick we could hardly move.

6. The onlookers were (stunned, amazed, surprised) by the vicious outburst.

7. Lincoln (repeated, argued, stressed) that he did not believe in bitterness.

8. People wept as the funeral (hymn, dirge, music) was played by the band.

9. The police had to (inch, pull, drag) the thief kicking and screaming.

10. "Be a good (kid, person, sport) and help your brother," the father said.

11. Working with paper can sometimes cause paper (slashes, slices, cuts).

12. Seeing a car (dash, race, dart) at the Indy 500 can be exciting.

13. The car engine (stalled, ceased, quit) in the intersection.

14. The food tasted (dull, bland, flat) and very dry.

15. Some consumer products are (reversed, repealed, recalled) when they're found to be defective.

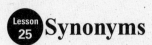 **Synonyms**

B. Vocabulary in Action

Replace each use of the words **revolt, rich,** and **sour** with the most appropriate synonym. Use the thesaurus entries to help you.

revolt: synonyms: *protest, disgust*

rich: synonyms: *wealthy, elegant, fertile*

sour: synonyms: *tart, rancid, crabby*

1. After her team lost the championship, Megan was in a <u>sour</u> mood.

   synonym: _____

2. Volcanic ash made the soil <u>rich</u>.

   synonym: _____

3. That company owner is a <u>rich</u> man.

   synonym: _____

4. The smell of the rotting meat will <u>revolt</u> you.

   synonym: _____

5. This lemon drink has a sharp, <u>sour</u> taste.

   synonym: _____

6. The colonists decided to <u>revolt</u> when the tax was imposed.

   synonym: _____

7. We toured the castle with its many <u>rich</u> furnishings.

   synonym: _____

8. The spoiled vegetables had a <u>sour</u> taste.

   synonym: _____

C. Vocabulary Challenge

Read each sentence and the three synonyms given for each. Choose the synonym that best fits each sentence and write it in the blank.

(*talk, recite, drone*)

1. Will you _____ at the poetry reading tonight?

   That boring speaker certainly does _____ on, doesn't he?

(*grab, retrieve, seize*)

2. A special device was used to _____ the ball from the water.

   I watched the hawk _____ the mouse and fly off.

(*walk, swagger, march*)

3. Let's take a _____ in the autumn leaves.

   He's so conceited he always seems to _____ around.

Antonyms

Teaching

An **antonym** is a word that means the opposite of another word. Antonyms are used when a writer wants to express contrasts.

My savings account is **barren,** while my brother's is **overflowing.**

One side of the family is **affluent**, while the other side is **poor.**

Marla values **honesty** in a person and is put off by **dishonesty.**

Antonyms, like synonyms, can have shades of meaning. Synonyms for *barren* include *sterile, ineffective,* and *useless,* each with a slightly different meaning. *Sterile* would be used to describe a land that does not grow crops, *ineffective* describes something that does not get results, and *useless* describes something with no value.

A. Antonyms in Action

Read each of the sentences. Look at the underlined word or phrase and then find an antonym in the list below that can be used to complete the sentence. Write the antonym on the line. Use a dictionary or thesaurus if needed. You will not use all the words.

honor	hoard	fearful	exhausted	frightened
pride	realistic	treacherous	forward	untamed

1. The pinto was <u>well trained</u>, but the mustang was wild and _____.

2. Unlike my <u>adventurous</u> brother, I have always been _____ of high places.

3. Several rafters, used to <u>safer</u> water, capsized in the _____ rapids.

4. You should feel _____, not <u>shame</u>, for what you did.

5. We forgot one of the supply bags, so the trail guide advised us to <u>share</u>, not _____, the food.

6. The force of the collision threw us <u>backward</u>, then _____ in the car.

7. I thought my excuse for being late was _____, but the teacher found it <u>unbelievable</u>.

8. We felt _____, not <u>full of energy</u>, at the end of the long climb.

9. Do not <u>disgrace</u> us by showing a lack of _____.

10. The child was so <u>excited</u> by the kitten, he _____ it away.

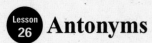 **Antonyms**   *More Practice*

B. Vocabulary in Action

Replace each use of the words **ridiculous, sorry,** and **sound** with the most appropriate antonym.

ridiculous: antonyms: *sensible, serious*

sorry: antonyms: *pleased, excellent, pleasant*

sound: antonyms: *damaged, unhealthy, unreliable, senseless*

1. The violent storm left what had been a <u>sound</u> house terribly _____.

2. Your argument for additional teachers isn't <u>ridiculous</u> at all; it seems very _____.

3. The former mayor was a <u>sorry</u> example of a public official, but the present mayor is

   _____.

4. Can't you stop acting <u>ridiculous</u> and be _____ for once?

5. Is the bank a <u>sound</u> place for investments, or is it _____?

6. Although his lungs are now very _____, they can become <u>sound</u> again if he quits smoking.

7. I am not <u>sorry</u> at all about your promotion; in fact, I am very _____.

8. All in all, we had a pretty _____ time at the party, very different from the last <u>sorry</u> event.

C. Vocabulary Challenge

Read each sentence and underline the two antonyms.

1. It seemed that everyone—friends, relatives, employees, enemies—was at the governor's inauguration.

2. The event opened with a stirring march and closed with a hymn.

3. In between, many speakers praised the governor's accomplishments and condemned those who opposed her.

4. In one of the best speeches of her career, the governor spoke about the need to support education, not just criticize it.

5. At the end of the speech, the once alert audience clapped enthusiastically, even though they were tired.

Denotation and Connotation

Many words have two kinds of meanings. The **denotation** of a word is its strict dictionary definition. The **connotation** of the same word includes all the feelings, both positive or negative, the word may bring to mind. Two words may have similar denotations but different connotations. Read these two sentences.

The *refugees* asked for help from the government.

The *fugitives* asked for help from the government.

The two words in italics have similar denotations. But *refugees* has the connotation of people fleeing persecution or war, while *fugitives* has the more negative connotation of persons who may have committed some crime.

A. Denotations and Connotations in Action

Read each pair of phrases and the words in italics. Write **P** in the blank if the word has a **positive** connotation and **N** if it has a **negative** connotation.

1. an *expensive* necklace _____

   an *overpriced* necklace _____

2. a *cunning* mind mind _____

   an *imaginative* mind _____

3. an *heroic* action _____

   a *rash* action _____

4. a parent's *burden* _____

   a parent's *responsibility* _____

5. creeping *warily* _____

   creeping *cautiously* _____

6. a *cool* manner _____

   an *insolent* manner _____

7 a *dramatic* performance _____

   a *hammy* performance _____

8. people *fleeing* _____

   people *escaping* _____

9. a day's *work* _____

   a day's *toil* _____

10. a wide *smirk* _____

    a wide *grin* _____

Lesson 27 Denotation and Connotation

More Practice

B. Vocabulary Words in Action

The italicized word in each sentence below has a **neutral** connotation—it has neither a positive nor a negative meaning. In each blank, write a synonym of the italicized word that has either a positive or a negative connotation as directed. Use a dictionary or a thesaurus if you need help.

1. Positive: The leading lady wore a *dressy* gown. _____

   Negative: The leading lady wore a *dressy* gown. _____

2. Positive: This plant has a strong *odor*. _____

   Negative: This plant has a strong *odor*. _____

3. Positive: The *building* burned in the fire. _____

   Negative: The *building* burned in the fire. _____

4. Positive: The tickets were *inexpensive*. _____

   Negative: The tickets were *inexpensive*. _____

5. Positive: What a *surprising* idea! _____

   Negative: What a *surprising* idea! _____

6. Positive: The boys were *resting*. _____

   Negative: The boys were *resting*. _____

7. Positive: He has a *modest* manner. _____

   Negative: He has a *modest* manner. _____

8. Positive: "I disagree," she said, *bluntly*. _____

   Negative: "I disagree," she said, *bluntly*. _____

C. Vocabulary Challenge

For each of the following words, find a synonym that has a more positive connotation. Then write a sentence using each synonym correctly. Use a dictionary or a thesaurus if you need help.

1. nosy _____ _____

2. odd _____ _____

3. sly _____ _____

4. risky _____ _____

5. fawning _____ _____

Using a Thesaurus

Lesson 28

Teaching

A **thesaurus** is a book of synonyms. A **synonym** is a word that has the same or similar meaning as another word. Some thesauruses also list **antonyms,** words that mean the opposite of another word.

> **speculate** *verb* **1. ponder, contemplate, meditate, reflect, think, cogitate, wonder** The philosopher speculated on the meaning of life. **2. conjecture, guess, surmise, suppose, infer, hypothesize, theorize** I'm speculating, but I think he will come to your party.

A thesaurus is arranged like a dictionary, with entry words in alphabetical order. The entry word usually is printed in boldface or colored type. The part of speech follows. The synonyms may also be printed in boldface. The entry word **speculate** has two basic meanings, shown here: "To think about something" and "to guess at something." How many synonyms are there for each meaning of **speculate?** (7) Often example sentences are given to illustrate the specific meaning of one or more of the synonyms.

A. A Thesaurus in Action

Answer the questions based on the thesaurus entries below.

> **benevolent** *adjective* **kind, kindhearted, kindly, good, goodhearted, altruistic** I felt benevolent when I helped with the holiday toy drive. ***Antonyms: malevolent, cruel, unkind**
>
> **flourish** *verb* **1. burgeon, bloom, blossom, grow, thrive, increase, prosper, wax** The roses flourished after I fertilized them. **2. wave, brandish, display, swing, sweep, flutter, wield, exhibit** My sister flourished her diploma with pride. ***nouns: embellishment, adornment, ornamentation, decoration, garnish, display** She signed her name with a flourish.

1. Which entry word is shown as two parts of speech? What are they?

_____

2. Which entry word is shown with antonyms?

_____

3. What is the direct antonym for the word **kind? benevolent?**

_____

4. What is the part of speech of the synonyms for the word **flourish** that means "to make broad, sweeping movement"? What is the number of the group for the word **flourish** that means "to grow well"?

_____

Lesson 28 **Using a Thesaurus**

B. Vocabulary Words in Action

common *adjective* **1. public, mutual** It is common knowledge that the dinosaurs are extinct. **2. widespread** Dandelions are a common weed. **3. typical** The doctor said that my type of knee injury is very common.

nice *adjective* **1. agreeable** To me, no flower smells as nice as a rose. **2. accurate** She does nice work repairing antique furniture. **3. respectable** His manners are not as nice as they could be.

plot *noun* **1. parcel** Grandpa has a small plot of land that he uses for a vegetable garden. **2. story** This book has an exciting plot. *verb* **1. conspire** The bandits were plotting to rob a bank.

Use the thesaurus entries above to choose a more exact synonym to replace each underlined word. Write each synonym in the space provided.

1. I figured out the climax of the <u>plot</u> almost immediately. _____

2. There used to be a <u>common</u> belief that fresh air was dangerous. _____

3. We appreciate the <u>nice</u> lettering on the sign. _____

4. Jake and I have a <u>common</u> interest in whales. _____

5. The three generals <u>plotted</u> to overthrow the czar. _____

6. This community park is for <u>common</u> use. _____

7. She has a personality that is not confrontational, but <u>nice</u>. _____

8. That misspelling is a <u>common</u> mistake. _____

9. She is not among the <u>nice</u> element of society. _____

10. The realtor was selling <u>plots</u> for development. _____

C. Vocabulary Challenge

Use the thesaurus entries above to find synonyms to replace the underlined words in each sentence.

1. Our <u>common</u> opinion in class was that the thief's character was <u>common</u>.

_____

2. We thought another character was too <u>nice</u> for the basic <u>plot</u>.

_____

3. Is it <u>nice</u> to state that the flu is a <u>public</u> problem?

_____

Name _____ Date _____

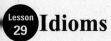

Idioms   *Teaching*

An **idiom** is an expression that has a meaning different from the meaning of its individual words. Read the two sentences below. One uses an idiom and one uses literal language.

> The flu had me feeling **under the weather.** (idiom)
> The flu had me feeling **tired and sickly.** (literal language)

Here are some other examples of idioms and their meanings:

Idiom	Meaning
all thumbs	very clumsy, especially with one's hands
get cold feet	become timid; be afraid of doing something new
on the ball	alert; intelligent; efficient
blow one's stack	get very angry

A. Idioms in Action

Read the words and phrases below and the sentences that follow. Complete each sentence by writing the letter of the literal word or phrase that has the same meaning as each underlined idiom.

A. were correct   E. fail or succeed   H. overjoyed
B. make him conceited F. ran   I. bankrupt
C. irritates me   G. learning how to ride J. visit
D. write or call

1. After we won the game, most of the fans were <u>walking on air</u>. _____

2. All this noise gets <u>on my nerves</u>. _____

3. I hope Jay will <u>stay in touch</u> when he moves to a different town. _____

4. We will <u>sink or swim</u> with this project; there's no in between. _____

5. The people who started up the new dot-com ended up <u>stone broke</u>. _____

6. My little sister is finally <u>getting the hang</u> of her new bicycle. _____

7. The escaped robbers suddenly <u>hightailed</u> it for the woods. _____

8. All the flattery began to <u>turn his head</u>. _____

9. I hate it when people <u>drop in</u> without calling first. _____

10. You <u>hit the nail on the head</u> with your answer to the third question. _____

 **Idioms**

B. Vocabulary in Action

Underline ten different idioms in the sentences below. Then define each one using the context of the sentence to help you.

1. Georgia has a green thumb and shares her vegetables with us.

   meaning: _____

2. Okay, give me your ear because I'm only going to say this once!

   meaning: _____

3. Pull up a chair and take a load off.

   meaning: _____

4. I think you will get your hands dirty if you get involved in that questionable business.

   meaning: _____

5. Get this straight, okay; I'm in charge of this project.

   meaning: _____

6. Rosa is really blue since her cat died.

   meaning: _____

7. Don't give me the runaround, just do the work on time.

   meaning: _____

8. It was hard to keep a straight face when Ken imitated the comic.

   meaning: _____

9. Alanna got the nod to play shortstop.

   meaning: _____

10. After a short rest I caught my second wind and continued the climb.

   meaning: _____

C. Vocabulary Challenge

Rewrite each sentence, replacing the underlined word or phrase with one of the following idioms. Then write a short meaning.

> on the tip of his tongue   getting my feet wet   under my belt   busy as a bee

1. Martin had the answer <u>ready</u>, but Lily said it first.

   idiom: _____

   meaning: _____

2. Leslie was <u>spending all her time</u> preparing for the holidays.

   idiom: _____

   meaning: _____

3. I'm just <u>getting ready</u>, so I'd like some tips about the job.

   idiom: _____

   meaning: _____

4. I felt better when I'd gotten a hot meal <u>inside me</u>.

   idiom: _____

   meaning: _____

Name _____ Date _____

 # Similes and Metaphors

Teaching

A **simile** is a comparison of two things that have something in common. A simile makes the comparison using either the word *like* or *as*. A **metaphor** is also a comparison of two things that have some quality in common. A metaphor does not use the words *like* or *as*, however.

Comparison	Characteristics	Example
Simile	with *like* or *as*	He growled like a bear.
Metaphor	without *like* or *as*	He was a bear in the morning.

A. Similes and Metaphors in Action

Underline the two items that are compared in each sentence. Then circle either *simile* or *metaphor*.

1. He had a spooky voice that made my blood feel like ice.

   (simile/metaphor)

2. As tall and skinny as a scarecrow, the hitchhiker stood there silently.

   (simile/metaphor)

3. The stars were beacons lighting up the night sky.

   (simile/metaphor)

4. The heavy rain was a gray wall blocking my view of the bridge.

   (simile/metaphor)

5. Like a plunging horse, my car jumped ahead quickly when I hit the gas.

   (simile/metaphor)

6. The lone desert monument was a sentinel standing guard.

   (simile/metaphor)

7. The road was as flat and deserted as a moon landscape.

   (simile/metaphor)

8. A large river moved like a snake across the prairie.

   (simile/metaphor)

9. The boy was a shadow, following her everywhere.

   (simile/metaphor)

10. A yard full of abandoned autos sat there like a fleet of metal soldiers.

    (simile/metaphor)

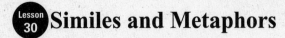

Similes and Metaphors

More Practice

Lesson 30

B. Vocabulary in Action

Underline the two items that are compared in each sentence. Circle a letter to identify the comparison as a simile (S) or metaphor (M). Then explain the meaning of the comparison.

1. The warehouse was a dusty, silent tomb. (S/M)

   meaning: _____

2. Alongside the river gleamed a green ribbon of meadow. (S/M)

   meaning: _____

3. My heart beat like a bass drum when the door burst open. (S/M)

   meaning: _____

4. The mosquitoes were little dive bombers attacking our skin. (S/M)

   meaning: _____

5. Ten birds lined up like bowling pins on the telephone wires. (S/M)

   meaning: _____

6. A carpet of snow covered the bricks we had unloaded yesterday. (S/M)

   meaning: _____

7. When I had the flu, my voice rasped like a creaky door. (S/M)

   meaning: _____

8. Butting each other's heads, the football players looked like goats. (S/M)

   meaning: _____

9. The floating log was a sunbathing platform for turtles. (S/M)

   meaning: _____

10. My kitten becomes a dancer when she thinks no one is looking. (S/M)

    meaning: _____

C. Vocabulary Challenge

Complete each sentence by writing a metaphor or simile as specified. Then write the meaning of each comparison.

1. Simile: After my fall, my legs felt like _____

   meaning: _____

2. metaphor: The tree was _____

   Meaning: _____

3. As light as _____, the heron landed on the lake.

   meaning: _____

Name _____ Date _____

Compound Words

Teaching

A compound noun is made of two or more smaller words. Compound nouns may be written in one of the following ways:

- joined as a single word: **outskirts   candlestick**
- as two or more separate words: **fairy tale   commander in chief**
- as a hyphenated word: **self-respect   father-in-law**

A. Compound Words in Action

Complete the chart below. First, write the smaller words that make up each compound. Then write the meaning of the compound word, using a dictionary as needed. Finally, choose an appropriate word from the chart to complete each sentence.

Word	Equation		Meaning
sunrise	_____	+ _____	_____
passers-by	_____	+ _____	_____
human being	_____	+ _____	_____
undergrowth	_____	+ _____	_____
jam puffs	_____	+ _____	_____

1. Leita baked wonderful _____ for her sister.

2. Several _____ witnessed the daring robbery.

3. We will leave on our hike at _____.

4. Many people are against the cloning of _____.

5. The dog heard rustling in the _____ and ran off to investigate.

Compound Words   *More Practice*

B. Vocabulary in Action

Add a word from the list to each word below to form a joined compound word.
Then write a sentence that uses each compound word correctly.

bud	block	ache	span	hopper
boat	top	fall	berry	hive

1. road_____ _____

2. wing_____ _____

3. mountain_____ _____

4. rain_____ _____

5. bee_____ _____

6. straw_____ _____

7. steam_____ _____

8. grass_____ _____

9. head_____ _____

10. rose_____ _____

C. Vocabulary Challenge

Remember that not all long words, or words that contain a noun, are compound
words. **Wonderland** is made up of two complete words (wonder + land), but
wonderful contains a complete word (wonder) plus a suffix (-ful). Separated
compounds can also be difficult to spot. One clue is to see if the two words are
often used together, such as **science fiction,** or **compact disk.** Underline each
compound word in this passage.

The repairman came today. He got our frantic hotline call about our

various non-working appliances. He fixed the toaster oven and the

dishwasher. He told us we needed a new microwave, and an icemaker for

the refrigerator. The stovetop clock would never work again, he said. "What

about the sink?" asked my mother, in a sorrowful voice. "I don't do

plumbing," he said sympathetically. "But my sister-in-law does. I'll give

you the number of her cell phone."

Name _____ Date _____

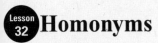

Lesson 32 **Homonyms**   *Teaching*

Homonyms are words that have the same spelling and pronunciation but
different meanings and often different origins.

Homonym	Sound	Meaning
founder¹	foun d(ə)r	(verb) to fail utterly; to collapse
founder²	foun d(ə)r	(noun) one who establishes something or the basis for something

The speeder stuttered out an excuse and then began to **founder.**

The **founder** of our organization will speak on Friday night.

When you are reading and you find a familiar word that does not seem to make
sense in the sentence, the word may be a homonym. Check your dictionary to
find the correct meaning.

A. Homonyms in Action

Circle the homonyms in each pair of sentences. Then write a brief definition of
each homonym. Use a dictionary if necessary.

1. The pitcher struck out five batters. _____

   Fill that pitcher with ice water. _____

2. Our dog food contains meat and corn meal. _____

   Lunch is my favorite meal of the day. _____

3. My corn hurts so badly I can't walk. _____

   Crows like to feed on the corn. _____

4. Hey, is this jacket yours or mine? _____

   There was an explosion at the coal mine. _____

5. That factory whistle makes a strange sound. _____

   This wobbly platform doesn't feel sound. _____

6. The neighbors' racket kept us up all night. _____

   May I borrow your tennis racket? _____

7. The otters slid down the bank into the water. _____

   The bank will lend us money for the business. _____

8. You can have the rest of the pizza. _____

   The workers took a rest to eat their lunch. _____

9. The witness was warned not to lie on the stand. _____

   Our dog likes to lie in the raked leaves. _____

10. The weight of my backpack causes me to stoop. _____

    Many families sit on their stoop in the evening. _____

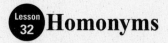 Homonyms

B. Vocabulary in Action

Pick a homonym from the word bank below that makes sense in each pair of sentences. Use a dictionary if you need help.

bat   lump   school   stick   felt   bow   pick

1. These stamps don't _____ very well.

   Use this _____ to prop open the window.

2. I _____ bad after our team lost the finals.

   We used blue _____ to make a flag.

3. Ramon and I go to the same high _____.

   The shark chased a _____ of fish to get his meal.

4. The hikers watched a swarm of _____ leave the cave.

   Put the _____, balls, and gloves in the locker room.

5. Have you seen the _____ to my guitar?

   I hope the team captain will _____ me for shortstop.

6. The king gave a formal _____ to the princess.

   I like to sit in the _____ of the sailboat.

C. Vocabulary Challenge

Read the definitions of the homonyms below. Then use each homonym correctly in a sentence. Use a dictionary for assistance.

1. Homonyms: *pore/pore*
   ({verb} to read or study carefully/ {noun} a small opening in the skin)

   _____

   _____

2. Homonyms: *fan/fan*
   ({noun} a device to create a breeze/ {noun} an enthusiastic supporter)

   _____

   _____

3. Homonyms: *drove/drove*
   ({verb} past tense of <u>drive</u>/{noun} a herd of sheep or cattle moving together)

   _____

   _____

Name _____ Date _____

Homophones and Easily Confused Words

Teaching

Homophones are words that sound alike but have different meanings and different spellings. When you write, you need to make sure you are using the form of the word that fits the sentence.

Homophone	Sound	Meaning
principal	prin s(ə) p(ə)l	head of a school
principle	prin s(ə) p(ə)l	rule of behavior, moral

The **principal** of our school introduced the assembly.

Jake's main **principle** is to be loyal to his friends.

A. Homophones in Action

ant/aunt	would/wood	there/their	rode/road
not/knot	break/brake	weather/whether	plain/plane

Use a pair of homophones to complete each sentence below. Use context clues to decide which word fits into each blank.

1. My _____ built a large _____ farm for the children's museum.

2. Use the _____ on your bike carefully, or you'll _____ your neck!

3. Do you know _____ the _____ will be sunny?

4. _____ you please help me move this pile of _____?

5. We _____ the horses up to a busy _____, but they refused to cross.

6. I can _____ tie that complicated kind of _____.

7. Will _____ be live music at _____ party?

8. The small _____ flew over the zebras on the grassy _____.

Homophones and Easily Confused Words

More Practice

B. Vocabulary in Action

Answer each riddle using pairs of homophones from the word bank below. Use a dictionary if necessary.

hoarse/horse	*ate/eight*	*weak/week*	*sail/sale*
dear/deer	*cruise/crews*	*pale/pail*	*flees/fleas*

1. What do you call groups of people employed on a vacation ship?

_____

2. What does your cat do when it runs away from itching insects?

_____

3. What do you call a beloved woodland animal?

_____

4. What do you call a discount offering on boating materials?

_____

5. What do you say after eating two-thirds of a dozen doughnuts?

_____

6. What do you call a grazing animal that has a sore throat?

_____

7. What do you have when you suffer from the flu for seven days?

_____

8. What do you have after you've spilled white paint all over the paint bucket?

_____

C. Vocabulary Challenge

Read the following passage. Circle six incorrect homophones. Write the correct examples on the lines below. Use a dictionary if necessary.

> Dear Sal: We require your presents at a party for hour sister, Jane. You may have herd that she one a scholarship to take a special coarse in science. Pleas bring a guest. Sincerely, the Adamses

_____ _____ _____

_____ _____ _____

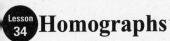

Homographs

Vocabulary

Many sets of English words are spelled the same but have different pronunciations and meanings. These sets of words are called **homographs,** from the Greek words *homos,* meaning "same," and *graphos,* meaning "written." They are often listed in separate numbered entries in the dictionary.

I tried to **console** my three-year-old sister when she lost her favorite toy.

We found the toy later, sitting on top of the television **console.**

Homograph	Pronunciation	Part of Speech	Meaning
console[1]	kən-sol	verb	to comfort; to try to relieve grief or sadness
console[2]	kŏn sōl	noun	a cabinet designed to hold a television set or radio

A. Identifying Homographs

Read aloud each pair of sentences. Circle the correct phonetic respelling of each bold-faced homograph. Use the pronunciation key below to help you. You may also use a dictionary if needed.

1. (lēd, lĕd)   My dog always likes to take the **lead** on our walks.

   (lēd, lĕd)   I'm so tired that I feel like my boots are full of **lead** weights.

2. (prŏ′ jĕkt, prō jĕkt′)   Mr. Evans assigned a **project** on Egypt to be due next month.

   (prŏ′ jĕkt, prō jĕkt′)   The machine that the movie theater uses to **project** films broke yesterday.

3. (mī-nōot′, mĭn′ ĭt)   Please wait—this will only take a **minute.**

   (mī-nōot′, mĭn′ ĭt)   During this experiment, we have to pay attention to the most **minute** details.

4. (prĕz′ ənt, prĭ-zĕnt′)   I wonder if James will give me a **present** for my birthday.

   (prĕz′ ənt, prĭ-zĕnt′)   Ellen will **present** the winner of the contest with the grand prize.

5. (rĕb′ ĕl, rĭ bĕl′)   The colonies decided to **rebel** against the British to obtain their rights.

   (rĕb′ ĕl, rĭ bĕl′)   Many people labeled Jason a **rebel** because he wore unusual clothes.

6. (ĭn-sĕns′, ĭn′ sĕns′)   The aroma of lavender **incense** gave the room a fresh feeling.

   (ĭn-sĕns′, ĭn′ sĕns′)   The judge was **incensed** by the defendant's outbursts in the courtroom.

7. (kŏm′ yōōn′, kə myōōn′)   My mother lived in a **commune** when she was a teenager.

   (kŏm′ yōōn′, kə myōōn′)   The monks often **commune** in the chapel before their daily work.

8. (kən vûrs′, kŏn′ vûrs′)   The most difficult aspect of foreign travel is being able to **converse**.

   (kən vûrs′, kŏn′ vûrs′)   To correct your hypothesis, place the last two components in **converse** order.

9. (pēkt, pē′ kĭd)   You are looking kind of **peaked**.

   (pēkt, pē′ kĭd)   For a traditional wizard's costume, you'll need a **peaked** hat with stars on it.

10. (kŏn′ tĕnt, kən-tĕnt′)   The **content** of your research paper is very sound.

    (kŏn′ tĕnt, kən-tĕnt′)   The principal felt **content** with the way he handled discipline at his school.

Pronunciation Guide

ă **p**at; oi **b**oy; ô **p**aw; th **th**in; ā **p**ay; ĭ **p**it; ou **ou**t; th **th**is; är **c**are; ī **p**ie; ŏŏ t**oo**k; hw **wh**ich; ä **f**ather; îr **p**ier; ōō b**oo**t; zh vi**s**ion; ĕ **p**et; ŏ **p**ot; ŭ **c**ut; ə **a**bout, it**e**m; ē **b**e; ō **t**oe; ûr **ur**ge; ♦ regionalism
Stress marks: ′ (primary); ′ (secondary), as in **dictionary** (dĭk′ shə-nĕr′ē)

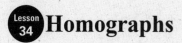 **Homographs**   *More Practice*

Lesson 34

B. Homographs in Action

Read the passage below. Circle the correct phonetic respelling of each bold-faced
homograph. Write a brief definition of each homograph. Use the pronunciation
key on the previous page and context clues to help you. You may also use a
dictionary if needed.

> We crossed the **desert** on our vacation last year. The trip was a **present** for my sister, who
> graduated from high school with honors. I didn't **object** because I wanted to see the desert
> birds and animals. While my sister counted the different kinds of cactus, I was **content** to
> identify the rock formations. Each night we **dove** into our dinners while our parents rested
> in the motel. While climbing a rock mesa one day, I got a deep **wound** on my hand.
>
> "I **refuse** to feel sorry for you," jeered my sister.
>
> "Now, just a **minute**—" I started to reply.
>
> "Kids, kids!" my father interrupted. "Do you want this argument to go into the
> photographic **record** of our trip?" My sister and I made a **compact** to stop quarreling.

1. (dĭ zûrt', dĕz-ərt') Meaning: _____

2. (prĕz' ənt, prĭ zĕnt') Meaning: _____

3. (əb-jĕkt', ŏb' jĭkt) Meaning: _____

4. (kŏn' tĕnt, kən tĕnt') Meaning: _____

5. (dōv, dŭv) Meaning: _____

6. (wōōnd, wŏŭnd) Meaning: _____

7. (rĕf' yōōs, rĭ-fyōōz') Meaning: _____

8. (mĭn' ĭt, mĭ nōōt') Meaning: _____

9. (rĭ kôrd', rĕk' kərd) Meaning: _____

10. (kŏm' păkt, kŏm păkt') Meaning: _____

C. Vocabulary Challenge

Choose a homograph from the word bank below to complete each sentence.
Then write a word that rhymes with the homograph. Use a dictionary if needed.

tear	*close*	*sow*
bear	*fly*	

3. _____ off the coupon at the dotted line.

Rhyming word: _____

1. I can't _____ to keep a secret.

Rhyming word: _____

2. Will the detective _____ the case soon?

Rhyming word: _____

Name _____ Date _____

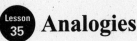

An **analogy** is a comparison of two dissimilar things which clarifies the less familiar one. In literature, it can be between unlikely pairs of items that are similar to each other in the same way. Or, it can be between two single items that clarify and reveal a character, feeling, incident, or thought. Analogies frequently occur in literature and science; you'll also find them on standardized tests. Read the examples below.

Whale is to **mammal** as **sequoia** is to **tree.**

WHALE: MAMMAL :: sequoia: tree

Each pair of words shows a relationship of item to category. Whale is a mammal just as sequoia is a tree. Notice that : stands for "is to" and :: stands for "as."

Type of Analogy	Example	Relationship
Part to Whole	WHEEL : BICYCLE	is part of
Synonyms	NAIVE : INNOCENT	means the same as
Antonyms	FRIEND : ENEMY	means the opposite of
Item to Category	HUSKY : DOG	is a type of
Worker to Tool	FARMER : COMBINE	works with
Grammar	CREEP : CREPT	is grammatically related to
Cause to Effect	PANIC : STAMPEDE	results in or leads to
Degree of Intensity	FEAR : TERROR	is less or more intense than
Object to its Material	TIRE : RUBBER	is made of
Product to Source	HONEY : BEES	comes from

A. Analogies in Action

Write the word from the bank that best completes each analogy. Then identify the relationship expressed by the analogy, using the chart for help.

cow	struck	dive	pan	wheel
whisper	fall	petroleum	bleed	antlers

1. FINGER : HAND :: spoke : _____   Type: _____

2. MINER : PICK :: cook : _____   Type: _____

3. FREEZE : FROZE :: strike : _____   Type: _____

4. PAPER : WOOD :: plastic : _____   Type: _____

5. EGG : CHICKEN :: milk : _____   Type: _____

6. DRAG : PUSH :: rise : _____   Type: _____

7. COLD : SNEEZE :: cut : _____   Type: _____

8. NAVIGATE : GUIDE :: plunge : _____   Type: _____

9. YELL : ROAR :: murmur : _____   Type: _____

10. BULL : HORNS :: moose : _____   Type: _____

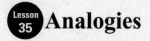

Analogies

B. Vocabulary in Action

Circle the word in parentheses that best completes each analogy. Then identify the relationship expressed by the analogy. Use the chart on the previous page to help you.

1. PLUMBER : WRENCH :: painter :
   (mural, brush, easel)

   Type: _____

2. RICH : POOR :: brave :
   (soldier, moneyless, cowardly)

   Type: _____

3. WINDOW : HOUSE :: chapter :
   (novel, library, dictionary)

   Type: _____

4. BERING : SEA :: Canada :
   (northwest, country, arctic)

   Type: _____

5. SECOND : MINUTE :: week :
   (Saturday, month, day)

   Type: _____

6. SPEND : SPENT :: sweep :
   (broom, swipe, swept)

   Type: _____

7. STRAIGHT : CROOKED :: black :
   (white, snow, river)

   Type: _____

8. MUSICIAN : INSTRUMENT :: writer :
   (pen, book, table)

   Type: _____

9. DOG : MAMMAL :: lizard :
   (scaly, desert, reptile)

   Type: _____

10. WHISPER: YELL :: simmer :
    (boil, heat, stew)

    Type: _____

C. Vocabulary Challenge

Underline the the two items that are compared below. Then write the meaning of the comparison in the space provided.

1. Placing Jack and Julie in the same room is like mixing vinegar and baking soda, acid and base.

   Meaning: _____

2. The old saying that the apple falls close to the tree was especially true in the case of Joshua whose father had been a child prodigy on the violin.

   Meaning: _____

3. Improvisational jazz is like cooking without a recipe. You take the musicians and instruments you've got on hand, let them warm up, then see how they play together.

   Meaning: _____

4. Kristen and her mother filled jar after jar with fresh sauce made from their home-grown tomatoes. Lining the cupboard shelves with tomato sauce was like putting money in a savings account.

   Meaning: _____

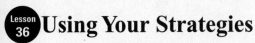

Using Your Strategies

Lesson 36

You have learned several basic strategies for figuring out a word's meaning:

> using the dictionary
>
> using context clues (general, restatement, definition, comparison, contrast, example)
>
> analyzing word parts (bases, roots, affixes)
>
> considering the meaning of related words.

Using a dictionary to learn the meaning of a new word is a good strategy for building your vocabulary. However, looking up a word means interrupting your reading. The other three strategies—using context clues, analyzing word parts, and learning from related words—can help you predict the meanings of new words *while* you read. You can look up the definitions later if you still need help.

A. Vocabulary Strategies in Action: Fiction

Read the following paragraph. Figure out what the underlined words mean using the strategies listed above. Then fill in the answers and circle the strategy or strategies you used.

> Last spring I found a kitten with long whiskers and fur the color of <u>ebony,</u> dark as the night sky. The kitten was purring loudly, so I figured it was hungry. I let kitty in the house and fed him. I took him to my bedroom and within hours my <u>feline</u> friend was acting as if the bedroom was his and I was the guest. The first time I left the kitten alone, I returned to find the wastebasket knocked over and the contents <u>strewn</u> around. He was playing soccer with a small wad of paper. It was then that I knew my pet was <u>mischievous.</u> I decided to name him Mischief.
>
> A few days later, we visited a <u>veterinarian,</u> Dr. Allen. He gave Mischief a <u>thoroughgoing</u> examination and all his shots. Because of Dr. Allen's care and a lot of love, Mischief is a very healthy kitten—and still mischievous.

1. ebony   meaning: _____

    strategy: context   word parts   related word   dictionary

2. feline   meaning: _____

    strategy: context   word parts   related word   dictionary

3. strewn   meaning: _____

    strategy: context   word parts   related word   dictionary

4. mischievous   meaning: _____

    strategy: context   word parts   related word   dictionary

5. veterinarian   meaning: _____

    strategy: context   word parts   related word   dictionary

6. thoroughgoing   meaning: _____

    strategy: context   word parts   related word   dictionary

Lesson 36 Using Your Strategies

B. Using Vocabulary Strategies

Read the following paragraph. Write the meaning of each underlined word using the strategies listed above. Then circle the strategy or strategies you used.

Scientists are increasingly using a unique weapon to clean up polluted soil and <u>groundwater:</u> plants. Using plants to <u>decontaminate</u> toxic waste is cheaper and easier than most other methods. Plant roots can absorb lead and other harmful metals and store them in their roots. For example, ferns thrive on <u>arsenic.</u> Plants can also be raised in <u>greenhouses</u> where they are used to purify water.

Nevertheless, using plants is not simple. There are always many issues to <u>resolve</u> when trying something new. Moreover, despite its tremendous potential, at least one major <u>drawback</u> limits the use of plants to clean up the environment. That is the time it takes to grow plants and the time it takes for plants to work.

1. groundwater   meaning: _____

    strategy: context   word parts   related word   dictionary

2. decontaminate   meaning: _____

    strategy: context   word parts   related word   dictionary

3. arsenic   meaning: _____

    strategy: context   word parts   related word   dictionary

4. greenhouses   meaning: _____

    strategy: context   word parts   related word   dictionary

5. resolve   meaning: _____

    strategy: context   word parts   related word   dictionary

6. drawback   meaning: _____

    strategy: context   word parts   related word   dictionary

C. Using Vocabulary Strategies

Write a paragraph using the words listed below. Apply the vocabulary strategies you have learned when you create your sentences so that a classmate would have to use these strategies to understand the four words.

inspiration   *literary*   *strive*   *extraordinary*

Personal Word List

Use the space below and on the next pages to create a list of words you want to learn. Write the definition for each word and use it in a sentence to make sure you make the word your own.

_____

_____

_____

_____

_____

_____

_____

_____

_____

_____

_____

_____

_____

_____

_____

_____

_____

_____

_____

_____

_____

_____

Personal Word List (continued)

_____

_____

_____

_____

_____

_____

_____

_____

_____

_____

_____

_____

_____

_____

_____

_____

_____

_____

_____

_____

_____

Name _____ Date _____

Personal Word List (continued)

_____

_____

_____

_____

_____

_____

_____

_____

_____

_____

_____

_____

_____

_____

_____

_____

_____

_____

_____

_____

_____

_____

_____

_____

_____

_____

Personal Word List (continued)

_____

_____

_____

_____

_____

_____

_____

_____

_____

_____

_____

_____

_____

_____

_____

_____

_____

_____

_____

_____

_____

Academic Vocabulary

Academic Vocabulary Lessons

Lesson 1 Academic Words—History

abolition *n.* the ending of slavery.

emancipation *n.* the act of freeing from slavery.

proclamation *n.* an official public announcement; *Abraham Lincoln freed the slaves in the Emancipation Proclamation.* [Latin: prefix *pro-,* before, and root *clamare,* to cry out, and the suffix *-tion,* process of.]

secession *n.* formal withdrawal from an organization; *The cause of the Civil War was the secession of the Southern states from the United States.*

segregation *n.* the separation or isolation of racial or ethnic groups from each other. [Latin: prefix *se-,* apart, and root *greg,* herd, and the suffixes *-ate,* to act on, and *-ion,* process of.]

slavery *n.* the condition of people who are owned as property.

suffrage *n.* the right to vote.

unalienable *adj.* unable to be transferred, given up, or taken away.

Break It Down—segregation

	prefix	root	suffix	suffix
word part	se		ate	
meaning		herd		process of

A. Match each word with its definition. Write the letter of the matching word in the blank.

_____ 1. not able to be taken away or transferred

_____ 2. the separation of people by race or ethnic group

_____ 3. the right to vote

_____ 4. the ending of slavery

_____ 5. the condition of being owned as property

_____ 6. formal withdrawal from an organization

A. abolition

B. secession

C. segregation

D. slavery

E. suffrage

F. unalienable

B. Fill in each blank in the paragraph with the correct vocabulary word.

abolition   Emancipation Proclamation   secession   slavery   unalienable

On January 1, 1863, President Abraham Lincoln issued an offical public

announcement called the _____ to free

persons held as slaves. It was aimed only at states that were in rebellion and had

left the United States through _____. It set the stage for the

ending, or _____, of the system of _____. It also

set the stage for restoration of _____ rights for African Americans.

Academic Words—History

Lesson 2

amendment *n.* a change or addition made to a legal document. [Latin: prefix *e-*, out, and root *menda,* fault, and the suffix *-ment,* process of.]

constitution *n.* a statement of the principles and laws that govern a nation. [Latin: prefix *com-,* with, and root *statuere,* to set up, and the suffix *-ion,* act of.]

doctrine *n.* a statement of government policy; *The Monroe Doctrine is an important U.S. policy.*

majority *n.* more than half the total number.

parliamentary *adj.* having to do with the group that passes laws, or legislature; *Parliamentary elections are followed in the United Kingdom, but not in the United States.*

veto *n.* the power of a president to stop bills passed by Congress from becoming law; *v.* to prevent something from being acted on, to say "no" to.

Break It Down—amendment

prefix	root	noun suffix
word part →	⟩ **menda** ⟩	⟩
meaning →		process of

A. Write the letter of the vocabulary word that best completes each sentence.

_____ 1. Fifty-five out of 100 people equals
    a) a veto.
    b) a majority.
    c) a constitution.

_____ 2. A change to a legal document is
    a) a constitution.
    b) an amendment.
    c) a doctrine.

_____ 3. The document that states the laws that govern a country is its
    a) majority.
    b) veto.
    c) constitution.

_____ 4. A statement of government policy is
    a) a doctrine.
    b) a majority.
    c) a veto.

_____ 5. The power of a president to prevent Congress from passing a law is
    a) the veto.
    b) a doctrine.
    c) a majority.

_____ 6. A process having to do with the legislature of a country is
    a) its doctrine.
    b) parliamentary.
    c) its amendment.

B. Match each word with the situation that best describes it. Write the letter of the matching word in the blank.

A. *constitution*   B. *majority*   C. *parliamentary*   D. *veto*

_____ 1. One-third of the people in Oldtown did not vote for Janice Blair, but she was elected mayor anyway.

_____ 2. A new country writes a document describing its guiding principles.

_____ 3. A law that would lower the voting age does not pass because the president votes against it.

_____ 4. The lawmakers participate in a system that causes them to be elected so they can pass laws and legislature.

Academic Words—History

Lesson 3

Academic Vocabulary

assimilation *n.* the process where people new to a culture adopt the behaviors and attitudes of that culture.

conservation *n.* the act of carefully managing and protecting resources, preservation.

emigration *n.* the act of leaving a country to live somewhere else, departing.

immigration *n.* the act of coming to another country to live permanently, entering. [Latin: prefix *in-*, into, and root *migarre*, to migrate, and the suffixes *-ate*, to act on, and *-ion*, process of.]

industrialization *n.* the process of developing an economy based on making goods rather than farming. [from the Latin prefix *indu-*, in, and root *struere*, to build, and the suffixes *-ial*, like, *-ize*, to make, and *-ation*, process of.]

urbanization *n.* the process of becoming more like a city. [Latin: root *urbs*, city, and the suffixes *-an*, like, *-ize*, to make, and *-ation*, process of.]

Break It Down—industrialization

prefix	root	suffix	suffix	suffix
word part indu	struere		ize	
meaning		like	to make	process of

A. Match each word with its synonym. Write the letter of the matching word in the blank.

A. *assimilation*   B. *conservation*   C. *emigration*   D. *immigration*   E. *industrialization*   F. *urbanization*

_____ 1. developing an economy based on making goods

_____ 2. entering a country

_____ 3. preservation

_____ 4. community development

_____ 5. leaving a country

_____ 6. adopting a culture

B. Write the letter of the word or phrase that best completes each sentence.

_____ 1. **Industrialization** often results in

   a) an economy based on making goods.

   b) more farming.

   c) people leaving the country.

_____ 2. A process that might occur to people when they come to live in a new country is their _____ of the new culture.

   a) urbanization

   b) assimilation

   c) conservation

_____ 3. **Emigration** is the process of

   a) people leaving their home countries.

   b) building more cities.

   c) adopting another culture.

_____ 4. It may be necessary for a country to begin a policy of **conservation** after much _____ has taken place and resources are almost used up .

   a) emigration

   b) assimilation

   c) industrialization

Academic Words—History

Academic Vocabulary

affect *v.* to make a difference to or in; to influence. [Latin: prefix *ad-,* to, and root *facere,* to do.]

better *adv.* in a more excellent way; finer.

effect *n.* an event that follows as a result of a previous event; *v.* to bring about. [Latin: prefix *ex-,* from, and root *facere,* to do.]

future *n.* a time that is to come.

past *n.* a time gone by; *adv.* at an end; over.

worse *adv.* in a poorer or less good way.

Break It Down—affect

prefix	root
word part		**facere**
meaning	to	

A. Match each word with its synonym. Write the letter of the matching word in the blank.

A. *affect*   B. *better*   C. *effect*   D. *future*   E. *past*   F. *worse*

_____ 1. result

_____ 2. finer

_____ 3. over

_____ 4. to come

_____ 5. influence

_____ 6. poorer

B. Write the letter of the word or phrase that best answers each question.

_____ 1. Which pair of words are antonyms?
a) better/worse
b) future/present
c) affect/worse

_____ 2. If freeing the slaves was an **effect** of the Civil War, which event happened first?
a) the Civil War happened first
b) the slaves were freed first
c) the events happened at the same time

_____ 3. The Southern states thought that secession was _____ than staying in the Union.
a) worse
b) better
c) the same as

_____ 4. The Emancipation Proclamation's purpose was to _____ the situation of the slaves.
a) ignore
b) worsen
c) affect

_____ 5. When the **future** becomes the present, what does the present become?
a) the past
b) an effect
c) the future

_____ 6. The _____ is a time gone by.
a) future
b) present
c) past

Name _____ Date _____

axis *n.* one of the perpendicular lines in a coordinate system; the *x*-axis (horizontal line) and *y*-axis (vertical line).

bar graph *n.* a chart that compares quantities by showing them as rectangles whose height is the value being compared.

intercept *n.* the distance from the origin (0,0) on a graph to the point where a line crosses an axis; *v.* to include between two points or surfaces. [Latin: prefix *inter-*, between, and root *capere*, to seize.]

line graph *n.* a graph in which pairs of values of an independent and a dependent variable are plotted in a coordinate system and connected by a broken line. *The high temperature every day for a month is an example of a line graph.*

real numbers *n.* numbers that are rational (can be expressed as the quotient of two integers; $^2/_3$) or irrational (cannot be expressed as the quotient of two integers, and whose decimals continue forever without any repeating group of digit; *.31331333133331. . .*) and are not imaginary.

whole numbers *n.* numbers including positive or negative multiples of 1 and zero.

Break It Down–intercept

prefix	root
word part ⟩ [ ] ⟩	**capere**
meaning ⟩ between	[ ]

A. Match each word with its definition or example. Write the letter of the matching word in the blank.

A. *axis*   D. *line graph*
B. *bar graph*   E. *real numbers*
C. *intercept*   F. *whole numbers*

_____ 1. the point on a graph where a line crosses the *x* axis and *y* axis

_____ 2. 5, .8645723706 . . ., 2/3

_____ 3. the graph showing how a child's height changed over a year

_____ 4. the vertical line in a coordinate system

_____ 5. a chart with rectangles showing how many people visited three Web sites

_____ 6. -27, 0, 769, 14,668

B. Write **T** if the sentence is true and **F** if it is false.

_____ 1. **Whole numbers** include positive and negative numbers.

_____ 2. **Real numbers** can be rational or irrational.

_____ 3. A **line graph** and a **bar graph** are two different ways of comparing quantities.

_____ 4. An **axis** is a broken line that connects points on a graph.

_____ 5. The **intercept** on the *y*-axis of the graph of $y = x - 3$ is +3.

Lesson 6 Academic Words—Math

Academic Vocabulary

base *n.* a number or symbol that is multiplied by itself or raised to a power. *The base is 7 in 7^4 (7 x 7 x 7 x 7).*

formula *n.* a rule expressed in mathematical symbols. *The formula for area is $A = l \times w$ (area), and the formula for a right triangle is $a^2 + b^2 = c^2$.*

opposite *adj.* at two ends of a space or line. *The opposite angles in a right triangle equal 90 degrees.* [Latin: prefix *ob-*, against, and root *positus*, placed.]

power *n.* the number of times a symbol or number is multiplied by itself. *The exponent is 4 in 7^4 (7 x 7 x 7 x 7).*

story problem *n.* a mathematical problem that is stated in words rather than in symbols.

value *n.* a number assigned to a variable. *The value of x is 5, or x = 5, in the equation $x + y = 46$.*

Break It Down—opposite

prefix	root
word part →	→ **positus**
meaning → against	

A. Write the letter of the vocabulary word that best completes each sentence.

_____ 1. A number that is assigned to a variable is
a) a power.
b) an opposite.
c) a value.

_____ 2. The expression $E = mc^2$ is an example of
a) a formula.
b) a story problem.
c) data.

_____ 3. In a right triangle, the two angles that total 90 degrees are
a) a power.
b) data.
c) opposite.

_____ 4. In the expression $E = mc^2$, c is
a) a base.
b) a power.
c) a formula.

B. Match each word with its definition or example. Write the letter of the matching word in the blank.

_____ 1. $s = 4$ cm. in the equation $V = s^3$

_____ 2. 3 in the equation $V = s^3$

_____ 3. r in the equation $A = \pi r^2$

_____ 4. Ian sold four newspapers at $.35 each and two magazines at $1.75 each. How much money did he make?

A. base

B. power

C. story problem

D. value

Academic Words—Math

Academic Vocabulary

axiom *n.* a truth that needs no proof, an established law.

congruence *n.* the state of two geometric figures that when laid together can fill exactly the same space. [Latin: prefix *com-,* with, and root *gruere,* come together, and the suffix *-ence,* state of.]

data *n.* facts, information; singular, datum.

proof *n.* the process of showing by logical steps that a statement is true.

tangent *n.* a straight line that touches a curve at a point; *adj.* touching at a single point. [Latin: root *tangere,* to touch, and suffix *-ent,* condition of.]

theorem *n.* a formula or statement that can be proved.

Break It Down—congruence

prefix	root	suffix
com	**gruere**	
with		state of

word part ▶
meaning ▶

A. Write the letter of the word or phrase that best completes each sentence.

_____ 1. A **tangent**
   a) is a straight line that touches a curve at a point.
   b) has congruence.
   c) is an axiom.

_____ 2. **Data** are
   a) axioms.
   b) facts.
   c) theorems.

_____ 3. Geometric figures that have **congruence**
   a) are tangent to each other.
   b) can be proven to be true.
   c) fill the same space when laid together.

_____ 4. An **axiom**
   a) cannot be proved.
   b) needs no proof.
   c) is false until enough data have been collected.

_____ 5. The **proof** of a statement
   a) makes it data.
   b) involves showing that it is true.
   c) has congruence.

_____ 6. A **theorem** differs from an axiom because it
   a) has no tangents.
   b) has no data.
   c) must be proved true.

B. Write **T** if the sentence is true and **F** if it is false.

_____ 1. The **congruence** of two geometric figures fill the same space.

_____ 2. **Axioms** must be proved using data.

_____ 3. Parallel lines are **tangent** to each other.

_____ 4. A **proof** is a process that is assumed to be true.

_____ 5. **Theorems** are established laws.

_____ 6. **Data** are used to prove theorems.

Lesson 8 Academic Words—Math

dependent *adj.* having a value determined by something else. *In the equations y = 3x, y is the dependent variable.*

independent *adj.* having a value that is stated; not being determined by anything else. *In the equation y = 3x, x is the independent variable.* [Latin: prefixes *in-*, not, and *de-*, from, and root *pendere*, to hang, and the suffix *-ent*, condition of.]

many *adj.* a large but not specific number of something that can be divided into separate parts. *There were many people at the concert.*

much *adj.* a large but not specific amount of something that cannot be divided into separate parts. *There was much snow in the driveway.*

solution *n.* the answer to a problem; the values of variables that make an equation a true statement.

symbol *n.* something that stands for or is a sign of something else *The symbol = means "equals."* [Greek: prefix *syn-*, together, and root *ballein*, to throw.]

Break It Down–independent

prefix	prefix	root	adjective suffix
word part	**de**		**ent**
meaning not		to hang	

A. Match each word with its definition or example. Write the letter of the matching word in the blank.

A. *dependent*   B. *independent*   C. *many*   D. *much*   E. *solution*   F. *symbol*

_____ 1. $x = 32$ in the problem $x = 2^5$

_____ 2. y in the equation $x = 7y^5 + y^3$

_____ 3. pennies in $100

_____ 4. $>$ meaning "greater than"

_____ 5. x in the equation $x = 2y^3 + y^2$

_____ 6. snow in a blizzard

B. Write the letter of the word or phrase that best completes each sentence.

_____ 1. If a variable is **independent,** it
   a) is a symbol.
   b) has many parts.
   c) has a value that is not determined by another variable.

_____ 2. If you know that there is **much** of a substance, you know that the substance
   a) cannot be divided into individual parts.
   b) is independent.
   c) is a symbol.

_____ 3. If the equation $56 \div 4 = 14$ is true, then $\div$
   a) is a solution to the equation.
   b) is a symbol that means "divided by."
   c) is a dependent variable.

_____ 4. The word that has the closest meaning to **many,** is
   a) solution.
   b) dependent.
   c) much

Name _____ Date _____

Academic Words—Science

Academic Vocabulary

asteroid *n.* one of thousands of small celestial bodies that move around the Sun, with orbits between Mars and Jupiter. [Latin: root *aster,* star, and the Greek suffix *-oid,* like.]

comet *n.* a celestial body with a head that develops into a long tail pointing away from the sun when its orbit is closest to the sun. [Greek: root *kometes,* long-haired.]

magnitude *n.* the brightness of a star.

mass *n.* the amount of material in an object.

planet *n.* one of the nine celestial bodies in our solar system that revolves around the sun. [Greek: root *planasthai,* to wander.]

velocity *n.* speed and direction of movement.

Break It Down—asteroid

	root	suffix
word part	aster >	>
meaning		like

A. Match each word with its definition. Write the letter of the matching word in the blank.

_____ 1. a body that develops a long tail when it nears the sun

_____ 2. speed

_____ 3. brightness

_____ 4. volume

_____ 5. a small body that orbits between Jupiter and Mars

_____ 6. one of nine large bodies that orbits the sun

A. asteroid

B. comet

C. magnitude

D. mass

E. planet

F. velocity

B. Fill in each blank in the paragraph with the correct vocabulary word.

asteroid   comet   magnitude   mass   planet   velocity

In our solar system, one of the nine objects circling the sun is a

_____. One of the small bodies located between Mars and

Jupiter is an _____. The body with a long tail streaming away

from the sun could be a _____ whizzing by. These objects are

moving with such _____ that it's hard to believe, especially

when you think of their huge _____. You'll see bodies ranging

in _____, or brightness, from the flickering candle of a distant

star to the fiery furnace of our sun.

Lesson 10 Academic Words—Science

atom *n.* the smallest unit of an element, consisting of a central positively charged nucleus surrounded by negatively charged electrons.

electron *n.* an elementary particle with a negative electric charge.

isotopes *n.* two or more atoms with the same number of protons, but different numbers of neutrons. [Greek: prefix *iso-,* equal", and root *topos,* place, and the plural suffix -*s.*]

molecule *n.* the smallest unit of a substance that has the properties of the substance; a group of atoms.

neutron *n.* a particle that has no charge and is part of the nucleus (except hydrogen).

proton *n.* a particle with a positive electric charge that is part of the nucleus of all atoms.

Break It Down—isotope

prefix	root	suffix
word part iso	tope	
meaning	place	plural

A. Write the letter of the word or phrase that best completes each sentence.

_____ 1. A **molecule** is made up of
    a) a proton, a neutron, and an electron.
    b) a group of atoms.
    c) isotopes.

_____ 2. **Isotopes**
    a) have different numbers of atoms
    b) different numbers of electrons
    c) different numbers of neutrons

_____ 3. An **atom**
    a) has a nucleus.
    b) is the smallest unit of matter.
    c) all of the above

_____ 4. The particle with the opposite charge of an **electron** is
    a) a neutron.
    b) a proton.
    c) an isotope.

_____ 5. A **neutron** has a charge
    a) equal to two electrons.
    b) equal to two protons.
    c) of zero.

_____ 6. A **proton**
    a) has a positive charge.
    b) occupies the same space as an electron.
    c) makes up a molecule.

B. Write **T** if a sentence is true and **F** if it is false.

_____ 1. **Isotopes** have different electric charges.

_____ 2. **Molecules** are not made up of smaller particles.

_____ 3. **Atoms** are made up of protons, neutrons, and electrons.

_____ 4. The nucleus of an **atom** has a positive electric charge.

Academic Words—Science

Lesson 11

Academic Vocabulary

carbon *n.* element with atomic number 6, symbol C; a nonmetallic element that occurs in many inorganic and all organic compounds. [Latin: root *carbon,* coal.]

element *n.* one of the fundamental substances each of which is made up of atoms of only one kind.

hydrogen *n.* element with atomic number 1, symbol H; the simplest, lightest element, normally a gas that combines with oxygen to form water H_2O. [Greek: root *hydro,* water, and suffix *-gen,* producer.]

matter *n.* anything that has mass, or weight, and takes up space.

nitrogen *n.* element with atomic number 7, symbol N; a gas that makes up 78% of the atmosphere and occurs in all living tissues combined with other elements.

oxygen *n.* element with atomic number 8, symbol O; a gas that makes up 21% of the atmosphere and combines with hydrogen to form water (H_2O).

phosphorus *n.* element with atomic number 15, symbol P; a nonmetallic element of the nitrogen family that is used in matches and fireworks.

sulfur *n.* element with atomic number 16, symbol S; a nonmetallic element of the oxygen family that is contained in many proteins.

Break It Down–hydrogen

	root	suffix
word part	**hydro**	
meaning		producer

A. Match each word with its definition. Write the letter of the matching word in the blank.

A. *carbon*   B. *element*   C. *hydrogen*   D. *matter*   E. *oxygen*   F. *phosphorus*

_____ 1. the element that combines with hydrogen to form water

_____ 2. a natural substance made of atoms of only one kind

_____ 3. the lightest element

_____ 4. a substance that has weight and takes up space

_____ 5. the nonmetallic element in all organic compounds

_____ 6. the element with atomic number 15

B. Write the letter of the word or phrase that best completes each sentence.

_____ 1. The two elements that make up most of the atmosphere are
a) hydrogen and carbon.
b) hydrogen and oxygen.
c) nitrogen and oxygen.

_____ 2. One atom of oxygen combines with two atoms of _____ to form water.
a) carbon
b) nitrogen
c) hydrogen

_____ 3. The element that occurs in all organic compounds is
a) nitrogen.
b) carbon.
c) hydrogen.

_____ 4. All of the elements have
a) hydrogen.
b) sulfur.
c) matter.

Academic Words—Science

Lesson 12

Academic Vocabulary

compression *n.* making the size, or volume, of something smaller by squeezing it together. [Latin: prefix *com-*, together, and root *premere*, to press, and the suffix *-ion*, result of.]

conductivity *n.* the ability to transmit heat, electricity, or sound. [Latin: prefix *com-*, with, and root *ducere*, to lead, and the suffixes *-ive*, performing, and *-ity*, quality of.]

direction *n.* the path along which something is moving; the relationship of two points in space.

pressure *n.* a force applied evenly across a surface.

rate *n.* the quantity measured per unit with respect to another measured quantity *The measure of inches of rainfall per hour is a rate.*

tension *n.* a force that tends to stretch something.

Break It Down—conductivity

prefix	root	suffix	suffix
con	**ducere**		**ity**
		performing	

word part ▶
meaning ▶

A. Match each word with its definition or example. Write the letter of the matching word in the blank.

_____ 1. The ability to transmit heat.

_____ 2. The storm is approaching from the southeast.

_____ 3. The storm is traveling approximately 14 miles per hour.

_____ 4. A force applied to a surface.

_____ 5. You apply this to stretch a rubber band.

_____ 6. Crushing a can for the recycling bin.

A. compression

B. conductivity

C. direction

D. pressure

E. rate

F. tension

B. Write **T** if the sentence is true and **F** if it is false.

_____ 1. **Compression** involves a force making something smaller.

_____ 2. The **rate** a car is traveling is measured in miles per hour.

_____ 3. **Tension** and **pressure** are both forces.

_____ 4. The **direction** of an object is the speed it is traveling.

_____ 5. **Tension** makes objects smaller.

_____ 6. The ability to send mail is an example of **conductivity.**

Spelling

Spelling Lessons

Silent *e* words and suffixes

Lesson 1

Teaching

pleas**e**	+ ant	= pleas<u>ant</u>	observ**e**	+ ant	= observ<u>ant</u>
resembl**e**	+ ance	= resembl<u>ance</u>	guid**e**	+ ance	= guid<u>ance</u>
propos**e**	+ al	= propos<u>al</u>	rehears**e**	+ al	= rehears<u>al</u>
practic**e**	+ al	= practic<u>al</u>	glob**e**	+ al	= glob<u>al</u>
ignit**e**	+ ion	= ignit<u>ion</u>	indicat**e**	+ ion	= indicat<u>ion</u>
enclos**e**	+ ure	= enclos<u>ure</u>	legislat**e**	+ ure	= legislat<u>ure</u>
financ**e**	+ ial	= financ<u>ial</u>	rac**e**	+ ial	= rac<u>ial</u>
rescu**e**	+ ing	= rescu<u>ing</u>	argu**e**	+ ing	= argu<u>ing</u>
rais**e**	+ ing	= rais<u>ing</u>	writ**e**	+ ing	= writ<u>ing</u>
relat**e**	+ ive	= relat<u>ive</u>	cooperat**e**	+ ive	= cooperat<u>ive</u>

Lesson Generalization: A **suffix** is a word ending that changes the use of a word. When you add a suffix that begins with a vowel to a word that ends with a silent **e**, drop the final **e**.

A. Complete the following exercises.

1. What happens to a word's final **e** when a suffix beginning with a vowel is added?

_____

_____

2. Write all words from the word list that end in a suffix.

_____   _____   _____

_____   _____   _____

_____   _____   _____

_____   _____   _____

_____   _____   _____

_____   _____   _____

_____   _____

B. On a separate sheet of paper, alphabetize all words ending in a suffix.

Silent *e* words and suffixes

Lesson 1

More Practice

1. pleasant	6. enclosure	11. observant	16. legislature
2. resemblance	7. financial	12. guidance	17. racial
3. proposal	8. rescuing	13. rehearsal	18. arguing
4. practical	9. raising	14. global	19. writing
5. ignition	10. relative	15. indication	20. cooperative

A. Answer each question with a complete sentence that uses a word from the spelling list. Add a suffix to the underlined word to create the correct word.

1. Does Herb <u>resemble</u> his brother?

   _____

2. Has the cast begun to <u>rehearse</u> the play?

   _____

3. Did everyone on the team <u>cooperate</u>?

   _____

4. Is the person you phoned <u>related</u> to you?

   _____

5. Did Lana <u>propose</u> her idea at the last meeting?

   _____

6. Are you going to <u>raise</u> corn in your garden?

   _____

B. Write the base form of each word. Then add the suffix to the base form and write the related form. Remember to drop the final silent **e** of the base form.

1. pleasing _____ + ant _____

2. resembling _____ + ance _____

3. financed _____ + ial _____

4. legislating _____ + ure _____

5. guiding _____ + ance _____

6. argued _____ + ing _____

Lesson 2 Silent *e* words and more suffixes

Teaching

festive	festivity	festively
severe	severity	severely
time	timing	timely
love	loving	lovely
like	liking	likely
complete	completing	completely
definite	definition	definitely
intense	intensive	intensely
defense	defensive	defenseless
price	pricing	priceless
blame	blaming	blameless
age	aging	ageless
sense	sensory	senseless
confine	confining	confinement
endorse	endorsing	endorsement
measure	measuring	measurement
amuse	amusing	amusement
engage	engaging	engagement
state	stating	statement
achieve	achieving	achievement

Lesson Generalization: When you add a suffix that begins with a consonant to a word that ends in silent **e**, keep the final **e**. Drop the **e** if the suffix begins with a vowel.

A. Complete the following exercises.

1. What happens to the final **e** in a word when you add a suffix beginning with a consonant?

_____

2. What happens to the final **e** in a word when you add a suffix beginning with a vowel?

_____

3. On a separate sheet of paper write all words from the word list that have a suffix beginning with a consonant.

4. On a separate sheet of paper write all words from the word list that have a suffix beginning with a vowel.

B. On a separate sheet of paper create a word search using at least 20 words from the word list.

Silent *e* words and more suffixes

More Practice

1. festivity	6. completely	11. blaming	16. measurement
2. severely	7. definitely	12. aging	17. amusement
3. timing	8. intensive	13. senseless	18. engagement
4. lovely	9. defenseless	14. confining	19. stating
5. likely	10. pricing	15. endorsement	20. achieving

A. Write the base form of each word.

1. achievement _____   6. amusement _____

2. ageless _____   7. engagement _____

3. completely _____   8. blameless _____

4. confinement _____   9. measurement _____

5. timely _____   10. endorsement _____

B. Find 12 words from the spelling list in the word search puzzle. Words might be written up, down, forward, backward, or diagonally.

S	D	J	F	P	O	P	U	U	Y	S	L
S	S	E	L	E	S	N	E	F	E	D	M
E	B	Z	F	V	S	T	A	T	I	N	G
L	L	P	W	I	V	T	Q	T	Y	F	Z
E	A	F	C	O	N	F	I	N	I	N	G
S	M	B	A	C	H	I	E	V	I	N	G
N	I	G	N	I	M	I	T	Q	I	N	Z
E	N	D	O	R	S	E	M	E	N	T	Q
S	G	N	I	C	I	R	P	D	L	J	Y
F	T	N	E	M	E	S	U	M	A	Y	C

Lesson 3 # Words ending *ate/ion*

equate	+ ion	= equation	evaluate	+ ion	= evaluation
separate	+ ion	= separation	create	+ ion	= creation
narrate	+ ion	= narration	navigate	+ ion	= navigation
decorate	+ ion	= decoration	coordinate	+ ion	= coordination
hibernate	+ ion	= hibernation	evacuate	+ ion	= evacuation
legislate	+ ion	= legislation	generate	+ ion	= generation
inflate	+ ion	= inflation	manipulate	+ ion	= manipulation
irritate	+ ion	= irritation	dominate	+ ion	= domination
obligate	+ ion	= obligation	participate	+ ion	= participation
congregate	+ ion	= congregation	isolate	+ ion	= isolation

Lesson Generalization: A word that describes an action is a **verb**: *decorate.* A word that names something is a **noun**: *decoration.*

> **ate** is a verb ending.   **ion** is a noun ending.

The word ending pronounced **/shun/** is usually spelled **tion.** Many verbs that end with **ate** can be changed to nouns by adding the suffix **ion.** The hard **t** in **ate** becomes a soft **t** in **tion.**

A. Complete the following exercises.

1. The **ion** ending makes a word a _____ .

2. Write the **ion** words from the word list.

_____ _____ _____

_____ _____ _____

_____ _____ _____

_____ _____ _____

_____ _____ _____

_____ _____ _____

_____ _____

B. On a separate sheet of paper, write a story. Use at least 12 **ion** words from the word list.

Lesson 3 Words ending *ate/ion*

More Practice

1. equation	6. legislation	11. evaluation	16. generation
2. separation	7. inflation	12. creation	17. manipulation
3. narration	8. irritation	13. navigation	18. domination
4. decoration	9. obligation	14. coordination	19. participation
5. hibernation	10. congregation	15. evacuation	20. isolation

A. Unscramble the nouns in the first column. First circle the **ion** ending in each. It is not scrambled. Then unscramble the verbs in the second column. Circle the **ate** endings.

1. ticapionartpi _____

2. gotbionail _____

3. etihbnriona _____

4. nimdionoat _____

5. artegenion _____

6. soateil _____

7. vuelatea _____

8. aterec _____

9. panimateul _____

10. atenrar _____

B. Complete each pair of sentences with a noun form (**ion**) and a verb form (**ate**) of the same word from the word list.

1. Judges filled out _____ forms on each contestant.

   The teacher will _____ the results of the tests.

2. The soldier was awarded a _____ for bravery.

   Who will volunteer to _____ the gym for the party?

3. The lonely forest gave the campers a feeling of _____ .

   One avalanche can _____ that mountain village for months.

4. The magician baffled us with the clever _____ of his props.

   The machine operator must _____ those levers in a certain order.

5. Can you _____ the boat between those rocks?

   The co-pilot took over the _____ of the airplane.

6. Does the furnace _____ enough heat?

   What music did people of our grandparents' _____ listen to?

Lesson 4 Prefixes and base words

re + strain	= <u>re</u>strain	dis + satisfied	= <u>dis</u>satisfied
re + quest	= <u>re</u>quest	dis + charge	= <u>dis</u>charge
ex + plain	= <u>ex</u>plain	sub + standard	= <u>sub</u>standard
ex + change	= <u>ex</u>change	sub + committee	= <u>sub</u>committee
in + justice	= <u>in</u>justice	pre + historic	= <u>pre</u>historic
in + corporate	= <u>in</u>corporate	pre + judge	= <u>pre</u>judge
de + notation	= <u>de</u>notation	con + tribute	= <u>con</u>tribute
de + merit	= <u>de</u>merit	con + genial	= <u>con</u>genial
pro + claim	= <u>pro</u>claim	per + fume	= <u>per</u>fume
pro + portion	= <u>pro</u>portion	per + mission	= <u>per</u>mission

Lesson Generalization: A **prefix** is a group of letters added to the beginning of a word to make a word with a different meaning. A prefix can be added directly to a base word to form a new word with a different meaning. The spelling of the base word does not change when a prefix is added.

A. Complete the following exercises.

1. How does the addition of a prefix to a base word affect the spelling of the base word?

   _____

   _____

2. Write the words with their prefixes from the word list. Underline the prefix in each word.

   _____   _____   _____

   _____   _____   _____

   _____   _____   _____

   _____   _____   _____

   _____   _____   _____

   _____   _____

B. Look at each base word in the list above. Can you add another prefix from the list to make a different word? On a separate sheet of paper, write as many new words as you can. Compare your words with a partner's.

Prefixes and base words

More Practice

1. restrain	6. incorporate	11. dissatisfied	16. prejudge
2. request	7. denotation	12. discharge	17. contribute
3. explain	8. demerit	13. substandard	18. congenial
4. exchange	9. proclaim	14. subcommittee	19. perfume
5. injustice	10. proportion	15. prehistoric	20. permission

A. Write the spelling word that contains each smaller word. Do not repeat words.

1. mitt _____   5. sat _____   9. it _____

2. just _____   6. rate _____   10. his _____

3. aim _____   7. but _____   11. port _____

4. miss _____   8. on _____   12. rain _____

B. Complete this puzzle with words from the spelling list.

Across
1. consent
3. merge; combine with something else
6. not content
9. exact meaning of a word
10. agreeable

Down
1. to form an opinion before having facts
2. ask for
4. to give
5. pleasing fragrance
7. trade
8. a mark put against someone

Prefixes and roots

Teaching

re + cess + ion = re<u>cess</u>ion   ex + hibit   = ex<u>hibit</u>

pro + cess + ion = pro<u>cess</u>ion   in + hibit   = in<u>hibit</u>

con + cess + ion = con<u>cess</u>ion   pro + hibit   = pro<u>hibit</u>

con + stitut + ion = con<u>stitut</u>ion   de + ject + ion = de<u>ject</u>ion

sub + stitut + ion = sub<u>stitut</u>ion   re + ject + ion = re<u>ject</u>ion

in + stitut + ion = in<u>stitut</u>ion   pro + ject + ion = pro<u>ject</u>ion

re + flect + ion = re<u>flect</u>ion   per + suade   = per<u>suade</u>

in + flect + ion = in<u>flect</u>ion   dis + suade   = dis<u>suade</u>

per + spire   = per<u>spire</u>   pre + sume   = pre<u>sume</u>

in + spire   = in<u>spire</u>   con + sume   = con<u>sume</u>

Lesson Generalization: A **root** is a word part that cannot stand alone. It must be joined to other word parts to form words. A root can be joined with many different prefixes. Changing the prefix forms a new word with a different meaning.

The root **ject** means "to throw."

deject = to throw down   reject = to throw back   project = to throw forward

A. Complete the following exercises.

1. How does changing the prefix of a word affect the meaning of that word?

_____

2. Write the prefix/root word combinations from the word list. Underline the roots.

_____ _____ _____

_____ _____ _____

_____ _____ _____

3. Write the prefix/root/suffix word combinations. Underline the roots.

_____ _____ _____

_____ _____ _____

_____ _____ _____

_____ _____

B. On a separate sheet of paper write each spelling word. Then make a new word from each spelling word by adding, taking away, or changing a prefix or suffix.

Prefixes and roots

Lesson 5

1. recession	6. institution	11. exhibit	16. projection
2. procession	7. reflection	12. inhibit	17. persuade
3. concession	8. inflection	13. prohibit	18. dissuade
4. constitution	9. perspire	14. dejection	19. presume
5. substitution	10. inspire	15. rejection	20. consume

A. Complete each sentence with two spelling words that have the same root. Some words may be used more than once.

1. The writer had feelings of _____ when she received a

   _____ letter from her publisher.

2. The _____ of graduating students into the auditorium was solemn, but the

   _____ of the same group was noisy and cheerful.

3. I _____ you know that you should not _____ that
   entire cake.

4. The actor changed the _____ of his voice so that it was a better

   _____ of his character's mood.

5. If I can't _____ you from trying that skating stunt, can I at least

   _____ you to wear kneepads and a helmet?

6. Seeing those runners _____ does not _____ me to take
   up jogging.

7. Mark and Janelle bought popcorn at the _____ stand while they watched the

   _____ of marching bands.

8. Writing a _____ was the first order of business after the

   _____ of the new town council.

9. Travel costs may _____ bringing the _____ to other
   countries.

10. One council member called for the _____ of Plan A after reading a

    _____ of the expected costs.

B. On a separate sheet of paper use at least 12 words to create a word search puzzle. Trade puzzles with a partner. Who can find all 12 words first?

Lesson 6 Compound words and contractions

back + ground = background	two + thirds = two-thirds
half + back = halfback	forty + eight = forty-eight
net + work = network	audio + visual = audio-visual
score + board = scoreboard	left + handed = left-handed
room + mate = roommate	brothers + in-law = brothers-in-law
video + tape = videotape	they + are = they're
else + where = elsewhere	who + is = who's
other + wise = otherwise	have + not = haven't
who + ever = whoever	were + not = weren't
any + one = anyone	should + have = should've

Lesson Generalization: Complete words can be combined to form other words in several different ways. When two words are simply connected, with no changes in either word, the word formed is called a **compound word**. Words joined by a hyphen are another type of compound word. When an apostrophe is used to show that one or more letters have been omitted, the word is called a **contraction**.

A. Complete the following exercises.

1. A _____ is the joining of two words without any changes. Write examples of these words from the word list.

_____   _____   _____

_____   _____   _____

_____   _____   _____

_____

2. A _____ can also be formed by joining words with hyphens. Write examples of these words from the word list.

_____   _____   _____

_____   _____

3. In a _____ , missing letters of joined words are replaced by apostrophes. Write examples of these words from the word list.

_____   _____   _____

_____   _____

B. On a separate sheet of paper, write a short story using at least 12 words from the word list. Be sure to use both types of compound words and contractions in your story. Share your work with a partner or small group.

Compound words and contractions

Lesson 6

More Practice

1. background	6. videotape	11. two-thirds	16. they're
2. halfback	7. elsewhere	12. forty-eight	17. who's
3. network	8. otherwise	13. audio-visual	18. haven't
4. scoreboard	9. whoever	14. left-handed	19. weren't
5. roommate	10. anyone	15. brothers-in-law	20. should've

A. Find the two words in each sentence that can be combined to form a compound or contraction spelling word. Write the word.

1. where should else forty _____

2. who two back ever _____

3. have other not room _____

4. ground in back main _____

5. not any seven one _____

6. work some then net _____

7. am were no not _____

8. they even are can _____

9. visual have under audio _____

10. not mate room and _____

11. brothers not law in _____

12. some wise in other _____

13. is any few who _____

14. some half percent back _____

15. have many any should _____

16. can forty yes eight _____

B. On a separate sheet of paper write a sentence using each set of spelling words. You may use the words in any order.

1. scoreboard, should've, forty-eight
2. anyone, who's, left-handed
3. brothers-in-law, weren't, background
4. they're, two-thirds, elsewhere
5. audio-visual, haven't, videotape
6. whoever, roommate, otherwise

Silent letters   *Teaching*

desi**gn**er	sole**mn**
ali**gn**ment	colu**mn**
campai**gn**	conde**mn**
gnawed	autu**mn**
inde**bt**ed	qua**lm**s
dou**bt**ful	ca**lm**ly
psalms	plu**mb**ing
psychology	nu**mb**ed
spa**gh**etti	**rh**ythmic
ghetto	**rh**ymed

Lesson Generalization: A word's spelling may include a consonant pair in which one consonant is silent.

gn   bt   ps   gh   mn   lm   mb   rh

A. Complete the following exercises.

1. Say each word in the word list aloud. Then, for each letter combination listed below, write the letter that is silent.

gn _____   bt _____   ps _____

gh _____   lm _____   mb _____

rh _____   mn _____

2. Write the words from the word list with silent letter combinations. Circle the silent letter in each word.

_____   _____   _____

_____   _____   _____

_____   _____   _____

_____   _____   _____

_____   _____   _____

_____   _____

B. Create a word search puzzle using all 20 words from the spelling list. Trade puzzles with a partner. Work your partner's puzzle. How many of the spelling words can you find?

Lesson 7 Silent letters

More Practice

1. designer	6. doubtful	11. solemn	16. calmly
2. alignment	7. psalms	12. column	17. plumbing
3. campaign	8. psychology	13. condemn	18. numbed
4. gnawed	9. spaghetti	14. autumn	19. rhythmic
5. indebted	10. ghetto	15. qualms	20. rhymed

A. Complete the following exercises.

1. Write the five one-syllable words from the spelling list.

_____ _____ _____

_____ _____

2. Write the ten two-syllable spelling words. Draw a line between the syllables.

_____ _____ _____

_____ _____ _____

_____ _____ _____

_____

3. Write the four three-syllable words. Draw a line between the syllables.

_____ _____ _____

_____

4. Write the spelling word that remains. _____

How many syllables does it have? _____

B. The list below contains three spelling words and other words that are similar in meaning to those words. In the first row, write the spelling words. Under each spelling word, write the words from the list that are synonyms to that word.

somber	solemn	uncertain	unsure	serious
skeptical	serenely	questionable	placidly	peacefully
tranquilly	grave	earnest	doubtful	calmly

_____ _____ _____

_____ _____ _____

_____ _____ _____

_____ _____ _____

_____ _____ _____

Lesson 8 Review

Review

1. practical	9. participation	17. persuade	24. should've
2. relative	10. coordination	18. defenseless	25. two-thirds
3. rehearsal	11. separation	19. prohibit	26. designer
4. arguing	12. obligation	20. procession	27. doubtful
5. definition	13. dissatisfied	21. background	28. spaghetti
6. achievement	14. proportion	22. roommate	29. column
7. blaming	15. explain	23. they're	30. rhymed
8. perspire	16. injustice		

A. An analogy is a special way of showing how words are related to one another. Complete each analogy with a spelling word that makes the second pair of words go together in the same way as the first pair or words.

1. **like** is to **liking** as **blame** is to _____

2. **blame** is to **blameless** as **defense** is to _____

3. **operation** is to **cooperation** as **ordination** is to _____

4. **rescued** is to **argued** as **rescuing** is to _____

5. **garden** is to **gardener** as **design** is to _____

6. **whose** is to **who's** as **there** is to _____

7. **inspiration** is to **inspire** as **perspiration** is to _____

8. **satisfaction** is to **dissatisfaction** as **justice** is to _____

9. **measuring** is to **measurement** as **achieving** is to _____

10. **evacuate** is to **evacuation** as **obligate** is to _____

11. **surfboard** is to **boardwalk** as **halfback** is to _____

12. **propose** is to **proposal** as **rehearse** is to _____

13. **would have** is to **would've** as **should have** is to _____

14. **pleased** is to **displeased** as **satisfied** is to _____

15. **completely** is to **completion** as **separately** is to _____

B. On a separate sheet of paper, write complete sentences using the fifteen words not used in A. The number of sentences may vary, but all fifteen words must be used.

Lesson 8 Review

Review

A. Three words in each row follow the same spelling pattern. Circle the word that does not follow the pattern.

1. scoreboard	videotape	prehistoric	anyone
2. campaign	congregate	designer	condemn
3. projection	injustice	subcommittee	prejudge
4. narration	reflection	separation	navigation
5. likely	completely	severely	calmly
6. evaluate	otherwise	elsewhere	whoever
7. proposal	practical	congenial	rehearsal
8. alignment	amusement	endorsement	statement
9. consume	exchange	institution	exhibition
10. intensity	severity	solemnity	festivity

B. Complete each analogy with a word from the list.

halfback	perspire	accelerate	designer	persuade
discharge	measurement	doubtful	hymn	campaign
navigate	two-thirds	rehearsal	qualms	ignition

1. **cold** is to **shiver** as **heat** is to _____

2. **sure** is to **positive** as **uncertain** is to _____

3. **decrease** is to **increase** as **decelerate** is to _____

4. **building** is to **architect** as **clothes** is to _____

5. **whole** is to **ten** as **fraction** is to _____

6. **car** is to **drive** as **ship** is to _____

7. **innocent** is to **blameless** as **doubts** is to _____

8. **pounds** is to **weight** as **inches** is to _____

9. **school** is to **graduate** as **army** is to _____

10. **baseball** is to **pitcher** as **football** is to _____

11. **recite** is to **poem** as **sing** is to _____

12. **sport** is to **practice** as **drama** is to _____

13. **fire** is to **match** as **engine** is to _____

14. **voter** is to **choose** as **candidate** is to _____

15. **counselor** is to **advise** as **advertiser** is to _____

Final *y* words and suffixes

Teaching

sway	swaying	apply	applied
convey	conveyed	defy	defying
defray	defrayed	envy	envying
dismay	dismaying	tally	tallied
employ	employed	modify	modified
subway	subways	celebrity	celebrities
medley	medleys	century	centuries
attorney	attorneys	penalty	penalties
pulley	pulleys	gallery	galleries
decoy	decoys	agency	agencies

Lesson Generalization: If the letter before a final **y** is a vowel, do not change the **y** when you add a suffix.

If the letter before a final **y** is a consonant, change the **y** to **i** before you add any suffix except **ing**. The **y** never changes before **ing**.

A. Complete the following exercises.

1. When a vowel comes before a final **y,** what happens to the **y** when you add a suffix?

_____ Write the words from the spelling list that end in a vowel-**y** suffix combination.

_____   _____   _____

_____   _____   _____

_____   _____   _____

_____

2. When a consonant comes before a final **y**, what happens to the **y** when you add a suffix?

_____ What is the exception to this rule? _____
Write the words from the list that end in a consonant-**y** suffix combination. Put an **e** next to the words that are exceptions to this rule.

_____   _____   _____

_____   _____   _____

_____   _____   _____

_____

B. On a separate sheet of paper, use each word from column two and four in the word list in an original sentence. Share your sentences with a partner.

Final *y* words and suffixes

Lesson 9

More Practice

1. swaying	5. employed	9. pulleys	13. envying	17. centuries
2. conveyed	6. subways	10. decoys	14. tallied	18. penalties
3. defrayed	7. medleys	11. applied	15. modified	19. galleries
4. dismaying	8. attorneys	12. defying	16. celebrities	20. agencies

A. Change the underlined noun in each sentence to the plural form. Change the underlined verb to its **ed** or **ing** form, as in the spelling list. Note: When you use the **ing** form, you must also add **is** or **was** before the verb.

1. The insurance <u>agency</u> <u>employs</u> many people. _____   _____

2. Mr. Shaw's <u>decoy</u> <u>sways</u> gently on the pond. _____   _____

3. The <u>penalty</u> <u>dismays</u> the hockey player. _____   _____

4. Our art <u>gallery</u> <u>defrays</u> the cost of the exhibit. _____   _____

5. The <u>subway</u> <u>conveys</u> thousands of commuters. _____   _____

6. Which past <u>century</u> <u>defies</u> understanding? _____   _____

7. The <u>pulley</u> <u>modifies</u> the distribution of weight. _____   _____

8. The other <u>celebrity</u> <u>envies</u> the star of the show. _____   _____

9. The singers of the <u>medley</u> <u>apply</u> new words. _____   _____

10. Which firm's <u>attorney</u> <u>tallies</u> the results? _____   _____

B. Find and circle ten spelling words in the puzzle. Words can be found up, down, forward, backward, and diagonally.

D	P	M	V	T	A	L	L	I	E	D	H
E	I	E	V	C	H	P	Z	G	T	I	T
F	Z	S	N	P	O	Y	P	E	X	A	M
R	C	S	M	A	U	F	K	L	S	R	J
A	M	U	G	A	L	L	E	R	I	E	S
Y	L	B	Y	S	Y	T	L	U	P	E	B
E	A	W	X	A	T	I	I	E	G	W	D
D	W	A	T	T	O	R	N	E	Y	S	Z
U	S	Y	O	C	E	D	X	G	S	S	J
G	D	S	T	R	T	Q	N	B	A	M	N

Lesson 10 — Words ending with *al* + suffixes

Teaching

loc<u>ally</u>	locality	tot<u>ally</u>	totality	individu<u>ally</u>	individuality
fin<u>ally</u>	finality	ment<u>ally</u>	mentality	origin<u>ally</u>	originality
leg<u>ally</u>	legality	mor<u>ally</u>	morality	practic<u>ally</u>	practicality
equ<u>ally</u>	equality	nation<u>ally</u>	nationality	form<u>ally</u>	formality
fat<u>ally</u>	fatality	punctu<u>ally</u>	punctuality	technic<u>ally</u>	technicality
actu<u>ally</u>	actuality	gener<u>ally</u>	generality	sentiment<u>ally</u>	sentimentality
re<u>ally</u>	reality	person<u>ally</u>	personality		

Lesson Generalization: When you add the suffix **ly** to a word that ends with **al**, remember that one **l** belongs to the base word and the other **l** belongs to the suffix. Don't drop either of the **l**s: national + ly = nationally.

Remember the unstressed **a** by thinking of a related word in which the accent is shifted to the syllable containing the **a**: for'mal-ly for-mal'i-ty.

A. Complete the following exercises.

1. When adding the **ly** suffix to an adjective to make an adverb, what happens to the spelling of the base word? _____ Write the **ly** words from the list.

_____   _____   _____

_____   _____   _____

_____   _____   _____

_____   _____   _____

_____   _____   _____

_____   _____   _____

_____   _____   _____

2. When adding the **ity** suffix to an adjective to make a noun, what happens to the spelling of the base word? _____ Write the **ity** words from the list.

_____   _____   _____

_____   _____   _____

_____   _____   _____

_____   _____   _____

_____   _____   _____

_____   _____

B. On a separate sheet of paper, write the **ly** words in alphabetical order.

Lesson 10 Words ending with *al* + suffixes

More Practice

1. locality	6. actually	11. nationally	16. originality
2. finally	7. really	12. punctuality	17. practically
3. legally	8. totally	13. generally	18. formality
4. equality	9. mentally	14. personality	19. technicality
5. fatality	10. morally	15. individually	20. sentimentality

A. Write the adverb **ly** or noun **ity** spelling word that is a synonym (S), a word similar in meaning, or antonym (A), a word opposite in meaning to the word listed.

1. completely (S) _____   7. site (S) _____

2. physically (A) _____   8. death (S) _____

3. lastly (S) _____   9. inequality (A) _____

4. promptly (S) _____   10. informality (A) _____

5. locally (A) _____   11. unreality (A) _____

6. lawfully (S) _____   12. detail (S) _____

B. Complete each analogy with a word from the spelling list.

1. **oak** is to **tree** as **specifically** is to _____

2. **body** is to **mind** as **physically** is to _____

3. **tall** is to **short** as **tardiness** is to _____

4. **sea** is to **ocean** as **indeed** is to _____

5. **jeans** is to **tuxedo** as **casualness** is to _____

6. **some** is to **all** as **partially** is to _____

7. **sport** is to **tennis** as **emotion** is to _____

8. **first** is to **last** as **originally** is to _____

9. **storm** is to **weather** as **outgoing** is to _____

10. **white** is to **black** as **copy** is to _____

11. **heavens** is to **sky** as **virtually** is to _____

12. **text** is to **script** as **ethically** is to _____

Words ending in *able/ible* or *ance/ence/ent*

Lesson 11

Teaching

depend	+ able	= dependable	com	+ pat	+ ible	= compatible
accept	+ able	= acceptable	sus	+ cept	+ ible	= susceptible
approach	+ able	= approachable	per	+ miss	+ ible	= permissible
obtain	+ able	= obtainable	im	+ poss	+ ible	= impossible
detect	+ able	= detectable	in	+ cred	+ ible	= incredible
clear	+ ance	= clearance	ex	+ peri	+ ence	= experience
resemble	+ ance	= resemblance	in	+ gredi	+ ent	= ingredient
ignore	+ ance	= ignorance	pro	+ min	+ ent	= prominent
comply	+ ance	= compliance	per	+ man	+ ent	= permanent
ally	+ ance	= alliance	ad	+ jac	+ ent	= adjacent

Lesson Generalization: The suffixes **able** and **ance** are more commonly added to complete words than to roots. The suffix **able** means "able to be" and is used to form adjectives. The suffix **ance** is added to verbs to form nouns.

The suffixes **ible**, **ence**, and **ent** are more commonly added to roots than to complete words. The suffix **ible** means "able to be" and is used to form adjectives. The suffix **ence** is a noun ending. The suffix **ent** can form adjectives in which the suffix means "having," "showing," or "being in the state or condition of."

A. Complete the following exercises.

1. Remember that the suffixes **able** and **ance** are more often added to _____

   than to _____. Write the **able** and **ance** words from the word list.

   _____   _____   _____

   _____   _____   _____

   _____   _____   _____

   _____

2. You will find that the suffixes **ible, ence,** and **ent** are more often added to

   _____ than to _____ . Write the list words

   that have these suffixes.

   _____   _____   _____

   _____   _____   _____

   _____   _____   _____

   _____

B. On a separate sheet of paper, scramble the letters of each spelling word. Do not scramble the suffixes. Trade papers with a partner. Who can unscramble all of the words first?

Words ending in *able/ible* or *ance/ence/ent*

Lesson 11

More Practice

1. dependable	5. detectable	9. compliance	13. permissible	17. ingredient
2. acceptable	6. clearance	10. alliance	14. impossible	18. prominent
3. approachable	7. resemblance	11. compatible	15. incredible	19. permanent
4. obtainable	8. ignorance	12. susceptible	16. experience	20. adjacent

A. Complete the crossword puzzle with words from the spelling list.

Across

2. unbelievable

5. next to

7. lack of knowledge

8. allowable

9. lasting

Down

1. able to get

2. a part

3. a moving out or away

4. not feasible

6. able to be discovered

B. Finish each incomplete spelling word with the correct ending.

1. The resembl_____ between the sisters are their promin_____ features.

2. The ambassadors hoped for a perman_____ alli_____ between the two compat_____ countries.

3. Being suscept_____ to colds is a nasty experi_____ .

4. A depend_____ and approach_____ person will make a more accept_____ candidate.

5. Compli_____ with that difficult rule was almost imposs_____ .

Lesson 12 Prepositional prefixes

Teaching

intermission	perennial	abdicate	paramedic
interview	percolate	absence	parallel
interstate	perforated	destruction	paraphrase
interpreter	perpetual	deprived	
interception	perseverance	depleted	
interrupt			
international			

Lesson Generalization: A **preposition** is a word that is positioned *before* its object to show the relationship between the object and another word in the sentence: **between, through, beside, from.** Prefixes often have the meaning of prepositions.

pre (before) + position = preposition

A. Complete the following exercises.

1. The prefix **inter** means "between." Write the words from the word list that begin with **inter**.

_____   _____   _____

_____   _____   _____

_____

2. The prefix **per** means "through." Write the words that begin with **per.**

_____   _____   _____

_____   _____

3. The prefixes **ab** and **de** mean "from." Write the words from the word list that begin with these prefixes.

_____   _____   _____

_____   _____

4. The prefix **para** means "beside." Write the words that begin with para.

_____   _____   _____

B. On a separate sheet of paper, write a short story that includes at least 12 words from the spelling list. Share your story with a partner or small group of classmates.

Lesson 12 **Prepositional prefixes**

1. intermission	6. interrupt	11. perennial	16. abdicate
2. interview	7. international	12. percolate	17. absence
3. interstate	8. paramedic	13. perforated	18. destruction
4. interpreter	9. parallel	14. perpetual	19. deprived
5. interception	10. paraphrase	15. perseverance	20. depleted

A. Write the spelling word that matches each definition. Underline the word in the definition that gives the meaning of the prefix of the spelling word.

1. a time of being away _____

2. between states _____

3. continued effort through difficulty _____

4. to have had things taken away from _____

5. time in between _____

6. reword the original _____

7. a coming between to stop _____

8. boil a liquid through _____

9. punched through _____

10. to rudely break in between _____

11. translator between languages _____

12. a tearing down _____

13. lasting throughout time _____

14. a conversation between people _____

15. step down from a high office _____

B. First cross out one letter in each syllable. Then join the remaining letters to form a spelling word.

1. part + call + gel

_____

2. cab + dice + mate

_____

3. perk + len + nic + alt

_____

4. rin + terp + nai + tpion + alt

_____

5. pair + ac + metd + yic

_____

6. deep + lent + red

_____

Lesson 13 The assimilated prefix *ad*

Teaching

de + celerate	= decelerate	ex + cuse	= excuse
ad + celerate	= accelerate	ad + cuse	= accuse
re + locate	= relocate	in + tention	= intention
ad + locate	= allocate	ad + tention	= attention
pro + gression	= progression	pro + nounce	= pronounce
ad + gression	= aggression	ad + nounce	= announce
de + rive	= derive	re + sent	= resent
ad + rive	= arrive	ad + sent	= assent
re + sume	= resume	com + prehend	= comprehend
ad + sume	= assume	ad + prehend	= apprehend

Lesson Generalization: When the last letter of a prefix changes to match the first letter of a root, the prefix is said to be assimilated.

ad + similat + ed = assimilated
(to) (same or similar) (made similar to)

The prefix **ad** is assimilated more often than any other prefix. It also causes more double-consonant spelling problems than any other prefix.

A. Complete the following exercises.

1. When the prefix **ad** is assimilated, it usually changes its **d** to the first letter of the base or root word it joins. Write the words from the spelling list that have assimilated the prefix **ad.** Circle the assimilated prefix in each.

_____   _____   _____

_____   _____   _____

_____   _____

_____   _____

2. Write the words from the list in which the prefix is not assimilated. Circle the prefix in each word.

_____   _____   _____

_____   _____   _____

_____   _____   _____

_____

B. On a separate sheet of paper, use each pair of words from the spelling list in an original sentence. Share your work with a partner.

Lesson 13 The assimilated prefix *ad*

More Practice

1. decelerate
2. accelerate
3. relocate
4. allocate
5. progression

6. aggression
7. derive
8. arrive
9. resume
10. assume

11. excuse
12. accuse
13. intention
14. attention
15. pronounce

16. announce
17. resent
18. assent
19. comprehend
20. apprehend

A. Complete each sentence with two spelling words that have the same root.

1. When you _____ the winners' names, _____ each name carefully.

2. A careful driver knows when to _____ and when to _____ .

3. We _____ much pleasure from watching the ships _____ at port.

4. Do you _____ the fact that I gave my _____ to the idea?

5. The city will _____ funds to _____ the historic building.

6. You should _____ that classes will _____ on schedule.

7. No one could _____ why it is taking so long to _____ the criminal.

8. Attracting so much _____ was not my _____ .

9. An unusual _____ of events finally led to an act of _____ .

10. Did Rick _____ you of making up an _____ ?

B. Read the meanings of the following roots. Then write the spelling words that contain these roots and match the definitions below.

gress—to go   **celer**—swift   **sen**—feel   **loc**—place

1. to move to a different <u>place</u>   _____

2. to go at a <u>swifter</u> speed   _____

3. to <u>feel</u> agreement with   _____

4. a <u>going</u> forward to attack   _____

5. to <u>feel</u> anger   _____

6. <u>place</u> or set apart for a purpose   _____

7. slow down from a <u>swift</u> speed   _____

8. a series <u>going</u> forward   _____

Hard and soft *c/g*

Teaching

citizen	cereal	courage	guard
concerned	certain	urgency	digestion
license	circumstances	magician	fragile
calendar	recycle	category	gymnasium
custom	reluctant	guarantee	gargle

Lesson Generalization: When the letters **c** and **g** have a soft sound, they are usually followed by an **e,** an **i,** or a **y.**

When the letters **c** and **g** have a hard sound, they are usually followed by the vowels **a, o,** or **u,** or by any consonant except **y.**

Many words end with the letters **cle** (recycle, miracle, vehicle) or **gle** (angle, jungle, untangle). Remember that the endings cannot be spelled **cel** or **gel** without changing the sound of **c** and **g.**

A. Complete the following exercises.

1. What letters usually follow a soft **c** or **g** sound? _____
   Write the words from the list that have *only a soft* **c** or **g**—no hard **c** or **g** sound.

   _____   _____   _____

   _____   _____   _____

   _____   _____   _____

2. What letters usually follow a hard **c** or **g** sound? _____
   Write the words from the list that have *only a hard* **c** or **g** sound.

   _____   _____   _____

   _____   _____   _____

   _____

3. Now write the words from the list that contain *both a soft and hard* **c** or **g** sound.

   _____   _____   _____

   _____

B. On a separate sheet of paper write the words from the spelling list in alphabetical order. Underline each soft **c** and **g** once. Underline each hard **c** and **g** twice.

Hard and soft *c/g*

Lesson 14

More Practice

1. citizen	6. cereal	11. courage	16. guard
2. concerned	7. certain	12. urgency	17. digestion
3. license	8. circumstances	13. magician	18. fragile
4. calendar	9. recycle	14. category	19. gymnasium
5. custom	10. reluctant	15. guarantee	20. gargle

A. Find the missing vowels in each word. Then write the word.

1. c_t_g_ry _____

2. c_r_ _ l _____

3. fr_g_l_ _____

4. c_t_z_n _____

5. g_ _rd _____

6. c_st_m _____

7. g_rgl_ _____

8. l_c_ns_ _____

9. _rg_nc_ _____

10. c_rt_ _n _____

11. g_mn_s_ _m _____

12. c_rc_mst_nc_s _____

13. c_l_nd_r _____

14. r_l_ct_nt _____

15. g_ _r_nt_ _ _____

16. m_g_c_ _n _____

17. c_nc_rn_d _____

18. r_c_cl_ _____

19. c_ _r_g_ _____

20. d_g_st_ _n _____

B. Find the spelling word that fits in the boxes.

1.

2.

3.

4.

5.

6.

7.

8.

9.

10.

11.

12.

13.

14.

Lesson 15 Indistinct vowels and related forms

Teaching

popular	popularity	ordinary	ordinarily	editor	editorial
regular	regularity	library	librarian	author	authority
solar	solarium	temporary	temporarily	superior	superiority
familiar	familiarity	secretary	secretarial	major	majority
similar	similarity	voluntary	voluntarily	minor	minority
		imaginary	imagination		
		necessary	necessarily		
history	historical				
victory	victorious				
memory	memorial				

Lesson Generalization: Unstressed vowels before the letter **r** are difficult
to identify. First, think of related forms in which the mystery vowel may be stressed.
Then use other clues to help you distinguish **ar/or** and **ary/ory:** The ending **ar**
often follows the letter **l**. The ordin<u>ary</u> **ary** is more common than **ory** and **ery**. The
ending **or** often refers to a person or occupation.

Both **or** and **ory** frequently follow the letter **t**. An unstressed vowel sound in the
middle of a three-syllable word is often dropped when the word is pronounced:
his-to-ry becomes **his-try**. Do not forget the unstressed syllable when you spell
these words.

A. Complete the following exercises.

1. The _____ ending often follows the letter **l**. The _____
   ending often refers to a person or occupation and frequently follows the letter **t**. Write the words
   from the list that have these endings.

   _____   _____   _____

   _____   _____   _____

   _____   _____   _____

   _____

2. The **ary** ending is more common than _____ or _____ .
   The **ory** ending often follows the letter **t**. Write the words from the list that have these endings.

   _____   _____   _____

   _____   _____   _____

   _____   _____   _____

   _____

B. On a separate sheet of paper use each pair of words from the list in a
sentence. Share your sentences with a partner.

Lesson 15 Indistinct vowels and related forms

More Practice

1. popular	6. editor	11. ordinary	16. imaginary
2. regular	7. author	12. library	17. necessary
3. solar	8. superior	13. temporary	18. history
4. familiar	9. major	14. secretary	19. victory
5. similar	10. minor	15. voluntary	20. memory

A. Unscramble the syllables of these spelling words. Write the words on the lines.

1. to ry sih _____

2. lar ims l _____

3. ppo u ral _____

4. op rra met y _____

5. ep ro ri us _____

6. im ron _____

7. tar nu olv y _____

8. to vci yr _____

9. lim air fa _____

10. cen ras y se _____

11. u egr lra _____

12. mag i i ran y _____

13. orj am _____

14. o yr emm _____

15. ral os _____

16. rrab y il _____

17. i rot de _____

18. id ran y or _____

19. er tar y sce _____

20. orth ua _____

B. The words in each group are related in some way. Write a spelling word that fits in each group.

1. everyday, usual, common _____

2. vital, essential, required _____

3. writer, novelist, columnist _____

4. superior, primary, leading _____

5. fanciful, unreal, mythical _____

6. conquest, win, triumph _____

7. approved, current, liked _____

8. atomic, electric, nuclear _____

9. unimportant, lesser, trivial _____

10. inferior, good, average _____

Lesson 16 Review

Review

1. employing	9. reality	17. absence	24. calendar
2. envied	10. approachable	18. accelerate	25. fragile
3. applying	11. ignorance	19. announce	26. gymnasium
4. attorneys	12. incredible	20. excuse	27. familiar
5. celebrities	13. permanent	21. resent	28. author
6. individually	14. interrupt	22. license	29. library
7. nationally	15. parallel	23. guarantee	30. necessary
8. equality	16. perforated		

A. Complete each analogy with a word from the spelling list.

1. **equality** is to **equally** as **individuality** is to _____

2. **sentiment** is to **sentimentally** as **nation** is to _____

3. **disruption** is to **disrupt** as **interruption** is to _____

4. **compliance** is to **complying** as **appliance** is to _____

5. **accept** is to **except** as **accuse** is to _____

6. **resemble** is to **resemblance** as **ignore** is to _____

7. **possibly** is to **possible** as **incredibly** is to _____

8. **present** is to **presence** as **absent** is to _____

9. **unequaled** is to **equal** as **unparalleled** is to _____

10. **actual** is to **actuality** as **equal** is to _____

11. **modify** is to **modified** as **envy** is to _____

12. **contain** is to **retain** as **consent** is to _____

13. **auto** is to **automobile** as **gym** is to _____

14. **real** is to **cereal** as **agile** is to _____

B. Complete the sentences with words from the spelling list.

1. After graduating from law school, the young _____ began

   _____ for jobs.

2. The firm considered _____ Dan because of he was so _____

   with their product.

3. After becoming famous, some _____ are no longer _____ .

Review

A. Three words in each row follow the same spelling pattern. Circle the word that does not follow the pattern.

1. citizen	cereal	custom	certain
2. absence	ignorance	experience	prominence
3. attorney	penalty	century	gallery
4. urgency	gymnasium	fragile	category
5. arrive	accuse	actual	announce
6. obtainable	impossible	dependable	detectable
7. reluctance	alliance	appliance	defiance
8. ordinarily	technically	temporarily	voluntarily
9. courageous	tallied	modified	envious
10. popularity	regularity	reality	similarity

B. Complete each analogy with a word from the list.

originally	imaginary	abdicate	fatality	major
interpreter	perpetual	superior	century	solar
percolate	attorneys	gallery	gargle	international

1. **small** is to **minor** as **large** is to _____

2. **medicine** is to **doctors** as **law** is to _____

3. **ten** is to **decade** as **hundred** is to _____

4. **last** is to **finally** as **first** is to _____

5. **president** is to **resign** as **king** is to _____

6. **Germany** is to **national** as **Europe** is to _____

7. **nose** is to **blow** as **throat** is to _____

8. **drama** is to **theater** as **art** is to _____

9. **water** is to **boil** as **coffee** is to _____

10. **moon** is to **lunar** as **sun** is to _____

11. **below** is to **inferior** as **above** is to _____

12. **life** is to **vitality** as **death** is to _____

13. **yearly** is to **annual** as **forever** is to _____

14. **report** is to **real** as **fiction** is to _____

15. **writing** is to **translator** as **speech** is to _____

Lesson 17 · 1 + 1 + 1 words and VAC words

fit	fitting	occur	occurrence
thin	thinnest	recur	recurred
mad	madly	concur	concurred
throb	throbbed	regret	regrettable
sum	summary	acquit	acquittal
zip	zipper	equip	equipment
quit	quitting	annul	annulled
admit	admittance	commit	commitment
remit	remitted		
permit	permitted		
omit	omitting		
submit	submitting		

Lesson Generalization: A word that has **1** syllable, **1** vowel, and **1** final consonant is called a **1 + 1 + 1** word: fit. A word that has a single **v**owel in a final **a**ccented syllable with one final **c**onsonant is called a **VAC** word: ad-mit'. The first seven words in the first column are **1 + 1 + 1** words. The last thirteen in the first and third columns are **VAC** words.

Double the final consonant of a **1 + 1 + 1** word or a **VAC** word before a suffix that begins with a vowel. Do not double the final consonant before adding a suffix that begins with a consonant.

A. Complete the following exercises.

1. Double the final consonant of **1 + 1 + 1** and **VAC** words before adding a suffix beginning with a

   _____ . Write the words from the word list that follow this rule.

   _____   _____   _____

   _____   _____   _____

   _____   _____   _____

   _____   _____   _____

   _____   _____

   _____

2. If the suffix following a **1 + 1 + 1** or **VAC** word begins with a _____ , do not double the final consonant of the word. Write the list words that follow this rule.

   _____   _____   _____

B. On a separate sheet of paper, write a story using at least 15 words from the list. Share your story with a partner or a small group of classmates.

Lesson 17 *1 + 1 + 1* words and *VAC* words

More Practice

1. fitting	6. zipper	11. omitting	16. regrettable
2. thinnest	7. quitting	12. submitting	17. acquittal
3. madly	8. admittance	13. occurrence	18. equipment
4. throbbed	9. remitted	14. recurred	19. annulled
5. summary	10. permitted	15. concurred	20. commitment

A. Form spelling words by adding the endings to the base words.

1. permit + ed _____
2. fit + ing _____
3. submit + ing _____
4. mad + ly _____
5. acquit + al _____
6. throb + ed _____
7. concur + ed _____
8. sum + ary _____
9. remit + ed _____
10. equip + ment _____

11. thin + est _____
12. annul + ed _____
13. zip + er _____
14. quit + ing _____
15. recur + ed _____
16. regret + able _____
17. omit + ing _____
18. admit + ance _____
19. occur + ence _____
20. commit + ment _____

B. Answer each riddle with two spelling words that rhyme.

1. What did the coach give the baseball team?

   a _____ to new _____

2. What was the tired tailor always planning?

   _____ the _____

3. What did the confused judge do?

   _____ what he had _____

4. What did the student consider when his homework was not completed on time?

   _____ the _____

5. What did the class decide when the storm hit again after they thought it was over?

   _____ that the storm had _____

Lesson 18 # Doubling final consonants

expel	expelled	profit	profiting
repel	repellent	benefit	benefited
propel	propeller	credit	credited
compel	compelling	edit	editor
dispel	dispelled	limit	limiting
refer	reference	model	modeled
infer	inferred	label	labeled
prefer	preference	travel	traveler
confer	conferring	cancel	canceling
transfer	transferred	quarrel	quarreling

Lesson Generalization: A **VAC** word must have a final accented syllable. Some **VAC** words have a form in which the accent shifts to a different syllable when the suffix is added. For these forms, do *not* double the final consonant of the base words when you add the suffix: con-fer' con'fer-ence.

A. Complete the following exercises.

1. A **VAC** word must have a final accented syllable. What happens to the final consonant when a

   suffix with a vowel is added? _____
   Write the words from the list that follow this pattern.

   _____   _____   _____

   _____   _____   _____

   _____   _____

2. What happens to **VAC** words when the accent shifts with the addition of a suffix beginning with a

   vowel? _____
   Write the words that follow this pattern.

   _____   _____

3. What happens to the final consonant of non-**VAC** words ending in a vowel/consonant combination

   when a suffix beginning with a vowel is added? _____
   Write the words from the list that follow this pattern.

   _____   _____   _____

   _____   _____   _____

   _____   _____   _____

   _____

B. On a separate sheet of paper, create a word search using at least 12 list words with suffixes. Trade papers with a partner. Who can find all the words first?

Doubling final consonants

More Practice

1. expelled
2. repellent
3. propeller
4. compelling
5. dispelled

6. reference
7. inferred
8. preference
9. conferring
10. transferred

11. profiting
12. benefited
13. credited
14. editor
15. limiting

16. modeled
17. labeled
18. traveler
19. canceling
20. quarreling

A. Add the endings shown to the base words and write the word forms. Follow the rules for adding suffixes to **VAC** and non-**VAC** words that you learned in this lesson.

1. quarrel + ed = _____ + ing = _____

2. refer + ed = _____ + ing = _____

3. profit + ed = _____ + ing = _____

4. infer + ed = _____ + ing = _____

5. travel + ed = _____ + er = _____

6. model + ed = _____ + ing = _____

7. confer + ed = _____ + ing = _____

8. propel + ed = _____ + er = _____

9. expel + ed = _____ + ing = _____

10. benefit + ed = _____ + ing = _____

11. prefer + ed = _____ + ing = _____

12. repel + ed = _____ + ent = _____

13. credit + ed = _____ + ing = _____

14. cancel + ed = _____ + ing = _____

15. edit + ed = _____ + or = _____

16. limit + ed = _____ + ing = _____

17. compel + ed = _____ + ing = _____

18. transfer + ed = _____ + ing = _____

19. label + ed = _____ + ing = _____

20. dispel + ed = _____ + ing = _____

B. On a separate sheet of paper create a crossword puzzle using at least eight words from the spelling list. Trade puzzles with a partner and solve your partner's puzzle.

Name _____ Date _____

Suffixes following hard and soft *c/g*

Teaching

elegant	navigable	ambiguous	extravagance
applicant	communicable	conspicuous	significance
intelligent	enforceable	contagious	vengeance
magnificent	replaceable	suspicious	negligence
	eligible	outrageous	innocence
	convincible		

Lesson Generalization: It is sometimes difficult to choose between the following endings when you are spelling a word: **ant/ent**, **able/ible**, **uous/ious**, **ance/ence**.

When the letters **c** and **g** have a hard sound, they will be followed by the vowels **a** or **u**. Use the endings **a**nce, **a**nt, **a**ble, **u**ous.

When the letters **c** and **g** have a soft sound, they will be followed by the vowels **e** or **i**. Use the endings **ence**, **ent**, **ible**, **ious**.

The final silent **e** is sometimes kept to protect the soft sound of **c** or **g** when a suffix is added.

A. Complete the following exercises.

1. Use the endings _____ , _____ , _____ ,

   and _____ when they follow a soft **c** or **g** sound. Write words from the list that follow this pattern.

   _____ _____ _____

   _____ _____ _____

   _____ _____

2. Use the endings _____ , _____ , _____ ,

   and _____ when they follow a hard **c** or **g** sound. Write words from the list that follow this pattern.

   _____ _____ _____

   _____ _____ _____

   _____ _____

3. The final silent **e** of the base word is sometimes kept to protect the soft sound of the **c** or **g** when a suffix is added. Write examples of this rule from the word list.

   _____ _____ _____

   _____

B. On a separate sheet of paper, write the words from the word list in alphabetical order.

Lesson 19 # Suffixes following hard and soft *c/g*   *More Practice*

1. elegant	6. significance	11. eligible	16. suspicious
2. extravagance	7. communicable	12. contagious	17. outrageous
3. navigable	8. conspicuous	13. magnificent	18. vengeance
4. ambiguous	9. intelligent	14. innocence	19. enforceable
5. applicant	10. negligence	15. convincible	20. replaceable

A. Find the missing vowels to complete each word. Write the word.

1. c__mm__n__c__bl__ _____

2. c__nt__g__ __ __s _____

3. c__nv__nc__bl__ _____

4. __l__g__nt _____

5. s__sp__c__ __ __s _____

6. __nf__rc __ __bl__ _____

7. s__gn__f__c__nc__ _____

8. m__gn__f__c__nt _____

9. __xtr__v__g__nc__ _____

10. v__ng__ __nc__ _____

B. Complete each sentence with a word from the spelling list.

1. Even the huge ship was barely _____ during the storm.

2. Susan groaned when she learned that the broken china was not _____ .

3. What is the _____ of the fifty stars in the American flag?

4. Are porpoises more or less _____ than dogs?

5. His bright red hair made the celebrity _____ in a crowd.

6. Ruth felt that hiring a band was an unnecessary _____ .

7. The police believe the new traffic law will be easily _____ .

8. Because of your _____ , the supplies will not arrive on time.

9. Each _____ for the job must submit a sample of his or her writing.

10. The directions he gave us were _____ and confusing.

11. Is your sister _____ for a college scholarship?

12. We had a _____ view of the mountains from our room.

13. The jury will decide the guilt or _____ of the accused.

14. Shana's idea is so wild and _____ that it just might work!

The prefixes *com* and *in*

Teaching

com + gressional	= congressional	in + tuition	= intuition
com + servative	= conservative	in + sulation	= insulation
com + notation	= connotation	in + nocent	= innocent
com + mentator	= commentator	in + munity	= immunity
com + mute	= commute	in + mortality	= immortality
com + mercial	= commercial	in + mediately	= immediately
com + petition	= competition	in + patient	= impatient
com + puter	= computer	in + postor	= impostor
com + promise	= compromise	in + peached	= impeached
com + bustion	= combustion	in + bedded	= imbedded

Lesson Generalization: A prefix may be spelled in several different ways.
The prefixes **com** and **in** follow the same spelling pattern. Both are spelled with
an **n** before most letters of the alphabet. Both are spelled with an **m** before
roots or words that begin with the letters **m**, **p**, or **b**. They are spelled this way
to make more compatible combinations that are easier to pronounce.

   Say **inmediately** and **immediately**.   Say **conmute** and **commute**.

Double consonants often result from joining prefixes and roots. Remember that
one consonant belongs to the prefix, and one belongs to the root.

A. Complete the following exercises.

1. The prefixes **com** and **in** are spelled with an **m** before roots or base words that begin with the

   letters _____ , _____ , and _____ .

   Write examples of this spelling pattern from the word list.

   _____   _____   _____

   _____   _____   _____

   _____   _____   _____

   _____   _____

2. The prefixes **com** and **in** are spelled with an **n** before roots or base words beginning with most
   other letters of the alphabet. Write examples of these words from the list.

   _____   _____   _____

   _____   _____   _____

B. On a separate sheet of paper, create a word search puzzle using at least ten words
from the list. Trade papers with a partner. Whose puzzle was the most difficult? Why?

Lesson 20 The prefixes *com* and *in*

More Practice

1. congressional	6. commercial	11. intuition	16. immediately
2. conservative	7. competition	12. insulation	17. impatient
3. connotation	8. computer	13. innocent	18. impostor
4. commentator	9. compromise	14. immunity	19. impeached
5. commute	10. combustion	15. immortality	20. imbedded

A. Unscramble each letter group and write the spelling word. First find and circle the form of the prefix **com** or **in,** which is not scrambled.

1. sporimot _____

2. upcomret _____

3. comumet _____

4. niotintiu _____

5. subcomnoti _____

6. nnoincet _____

7. verseconivat _____

8. dddeimbe _____

9. lateiymedim _____

10. cheapimde _____

11. camecomril _____

12. semporcomi _____

13. talusinino _____

14. saloniconserg _____

15. nutimimy _____

16. notitepicom _____

17. tapimniet _____

18. ononconitat _____

19. taromimlyit _____

20. tentramcomo _____

B. Improve each sentence by leaving out the unnecessary words. Rewrite the improved sentence and underline the spelling word in each.

1. What I mean is the computer is a valuable machine.

_____

2. Carlo will be the commentator and the reason is because he is a clever speaker.

_____

3. War was avoided because of the fact that both countries agreed to compromise.

_____

4. What I think is that the senator should not be impeached.

_____

5. The thing is, this vaccine provides immunity from polio.

_____

6. What I went to the doctor for was to have this imbedded splinter removed.

_____

Name _____ Date _____

Lesson 21 **More assimilated prefixes**   *Teaching*

ad + ford	= afford	com + respondent	= correspondent
ad + fliction	= affliction	com + rupt	= corrupt
ad + firmative	= affirmative	in + responsible	= irresponsible
ad + fection	= affection	in + rigation	= irrigation
dis + ficult	= difficult	in + resistible	= irresistible
sub + fered	= suffered	com + lision	= collision
sub + focate	= suffocate	com + lapse	= collapse
sub + ficient	= sufficient	in + luminate	= illuminate
ob + ficial	= official	in + legible	= illegible
ob + fered	= offered	in + literate	= illiterate

Lesson Generalization: If prefixes were always added directly to a base word or root, some consonant combinations would be difficult to pronounce:

adford   disficult   subfocate   comrespond   comlapse

Assimilated prefixes solve pronunciation problems but sometimes cause spelling problems. Double consonants result when the last letter of the prefix changes to match the first letter of the root.

A. Complete the following exercises.

1. Look at the words in the first column. When a prefix is added to a root or base word beginning with the letter **f,** how does the prefix change? _____
Write the words from the list that follow this pattern.

_____   _____   _____

_____   _____   _____

_____   _____   _____

_____

2. Look at the words in the second column of the list. When the prefix **com** or **in** is added to a root or base word beginning with **r** or **l,** how does the prefix change? _____
Write the words from the list that follow this pattern.

_____   _____   _____

_____   _____   _____

_____   _____   _____

_____

B. On a separate sheet of paper, write the words from the list in alphabetical order.

Lesson 21 More assimilated prefixes

More Practice

1. afford	6. suffered	11. correspondent	16. collision
2. affliction	7. suffocate	12. corrupt	17. collapse
3. affirmative	8. sufficient	13. irresponsible	18. illuminate
4. affection	9. official	14. irrigation	19. illegible
5. difficult	10. offered	15. irresistible	20. illiterate

A. Find and circle the 15 spelling words in this word search puzzle. They are written forward, up, and down

```
I  R  R  E  S  P  O  N  S  I  B  L  E  I
R  C  O  L  L  A  P  S  E  L  A  A  V  L
R  T  E  B  C  M  R  U  N  L  F  I  I  L
E  L  T  I  H  V  U  F  G  I  F  C  T  U
S  U  A  G  W  Z  S  F  O  T  E  I  A  M
I  C  C  E  M  J  K  E  Y  E  C  F  M  I
S  I  O  L  U  M  B  R  T  R  T  F  R  N
T  F  F  L  D  C  H  E  K  A  I  O  I  A
I  F  F  I  R  S  U  D  T  T  O  X  F  T
B  I  U  L  O  H  M  Y  B  E  N  D  F  E
L  D  S  U  F  F  I  C  I  E  N  T  A  O
E  O  F  F  E  R  E  D  A  F  F  O  R  D
```

B. Find the misspelled word in each group. Write the word correctly.

1. irrigation	official	suffered	corespondent	_____
2. suffocate	difficult	afliction	afford	_____
3. collapse	corupt	illuminate	suffocate	_____
4. colision	affliction	illiterate	affection	_____
5. corrupted	irigation	sufficient	offered	_____
6. correspondent	irresistible	illuminate	ilegible	_____

The letters *qu*

Teaching

unique	acquire	quizzical
clique	acquainted	quiver
plaque	adequately	questionnaire
	colloquial	quarantine
masquerade	inquisitive	quench
conquer	banquet	quaint
lacquer	sequel	quintuplet

Lesson Generalization: The letter **q** is always followed by the letter **u** in the English language. In some words, **qu** is pronounced **/k/.** In most words, **qu** is pronounced **/kw/.**

When **qu** is pronounced **/k/,** it can appear in the middle of a word or at the end of a word: con**qu**er, pla**qu**e.

When **qu** is pronounced **/kw/,** it can appear in the middle of a word or at the beginning of a word: e**qu**ator, **qu**arrel.

The spelling is always **que** at the end of a word.

A. Complete the following exercises.

1. In most words, the letter combination **qu** is pronounced **/kw/.** It can appear at the beginning or

    _____ of a word. Write the words from the spelling list in which the **qu** letter combination is pronounced **/kw/.**

    _____   _____   _____

    _____   _____   _____

    _____   _____   _____

    _____   _____   _____

    _____   _____

2. When the **qu** letter combination appears at the end of a word, it has the **/k/** sound and is spelled **que.** Write the words in which **que** is pronounced **/k/.**

    _____   _____   _____

    _____   _____   _____

B. On a separate sheet of paper, write the words in the spelling list with a brief definition for each.

The letters *qu*

Lesson 22

More Practice

1. unique	6. lacquer	11. inquisitive	16. questionnaire
2. clique	7. acquire	12. banquet	17. quarantine
3. plaque	8. acquainted	13. sequel	18. quench
4. masquerade	9. adequately	14. quizzical	19. quaint
5. conquer	10. colloquial	15. quiver	20. quintuplet

A. The words in each group are related in some way. Write the spelling word that fits in each group.

1. twin   triplet   quadruplet   _____

2. sole   exclusive   only   _____

3. get   obtain   procure   _____

4. sufficiently   suitable   satisfactorily   _____

5. shake   tremble   shiver   _____

6. idiomatic   slang   informal   _____

7. feast   dinner   meal   _____

8. party   festival   gala   _____

9. group   association   club   _____

10. strange   unusual   eccentric   _____

11. defeat   overcome   subdue   _____

12. curious   quizzical   prying   _____

13. extinguish   satisfy   appease   _____

14. detention   isolation   restriction   _____

15. continuation   follow-up   installment   _____

16. tablet   marker   panel   _____

17. informed   known   familiar   _____

B. On a separate sheet of paper, first write in alphabetical order the spelling words that have the **/k/** sound. Then alphabetize the spelling words that have the **/kw/** sound.

Lesson 23 # The letter combinations *ph* and *gh*   *Teaching*

enough	phase	pamphlet	atmosphere
roughly	phantom	symphonic	hemisphere
toughness	pharmacy	triumphantly	decipher
laughter	physician	alphabetical	amphibian
coughed	philosophy	catastrophe	emphasize

Lesson Generalization: Any word in which the **/f/** sound is spelled with the letters **gh** comes from Old English.

Any word in which the **/f/** sound is spelled with the letters **ph** comes from the Greek language. Many of those words begin with the **ph** letter combination.

A. Complete the following exercises.

1. The letter combinations **gh** and **ph** both are pronounced _____ .

2. Write the words from the spelling list with the **gh** letter combination.

_____   _____   _____

_____   _____

3. Write the words from the spelling list with the **ph** letter combination.

_____   _____   _____

_____   _____   _____

_____   _____   _____

_____   _____   _____

_____   _____   _____

B. On a separate sheet of paper, create a word scramble using the words from the spelling list. Do not scramble the **ph** or **gh** letter combinations. Trade papers with a partner and try to solve your partner's word scramble.

Lesson 23 The letter combinations *ph* and *gh*

More Practice

1. enough
2. roughly
3. toughness
4. laughter
5. coughed

6. pamphlet
7. symphonic
8. triumphantly
9. alphabetical
10. catastrophe

11. phase
12. phantom
13. pharmacy
14. physician
15. philosophy

16. atmosphere
17. hemisphere
18. decipher
19. amphibian
20. emphasize

A. For each of the following book titles, find and circle the incorrectly spelled word from the spelling list. Then write the word correctly.

1. The Alfabetical Phase by A.B.C. Order   _____

2. Catastrophe in Our Hemispere by Pol R. Bear   _____

3. How to Deciher Codes by !$4CT, **=+##??   _____

4. My Mother the Fantom by I.M. Ghostly   _____

5. A Simphonic Atmosphere by Hum A. Long   _____

6. Does Football Emphsise Tackling? by U. Play Roughly   _____

7. A Little Lauhter by Minnie HaHa   _____

8. The Philosofy of Toughness by U.R.A. Pushover   _____

9. A Physician's Guide to Parmacy by Ann T.B. Otics   _____

10. Reptiles and Amfibians by Al E. Gator   _____

B. Find and circle ten words from the spelling list in this word search puzzle. Words are forward and backward.

G	U	P	A	M	P	H	L	E	T	Z	K
N	A	T	M	O	S	P	H	E	R	E	S
N	A	I	C	I	S	Y	H	P	P	T	W
O	K	D	E	H	G	U	O	C	I	S	O
E	E	R	E	H	P	S	I	M	E	H	F
T	R	I	U	M	P	H	A	N	T	L	Y
T	X	J	E	N	O	U	G	H	Y	W	W
E	H	P	O	R	T	S	A	T	A	C	J
T	V	Q	I	P	H	A	S	E	N	I	G
V	N	A	I	B	I	H	P	M	A	Z	O

Review

Review

1. regrettable	9. applicant	17. official	25. inquisitive
2. admitted	10. extravagance	18. difficult	26. enough
3. occurred	11. replaceable	19. collapse	27. pamphlet
4. equipment	12. outrageous	20. correspondent	28. physician
5. propeller	13. commercial	21. irresponsible	29. atmosphere
6. referring	14. immediately	22. unique	30. catastrophe
7. labeling	15. competition	23. conquer	
8. canceled	16. impatient	24. acquainted	

A. Complete each analogy with a word from the spelling list.

1. **prefer** is to **preferring** as **refer** is to _____

2. **assistance** is to **assisted** as **acquaintance** is to _____

3. **control** is to **controllable** as **regret** is to _____

4. **omit** is to **omitted** as **admit** is to _____

5. **editor** is to **edit** as **conqueror** is to _____

6. **definite** is to **definitely** as **immediate** is to _____

7. **travel** is to **traveled** as **cancel** is to _____

8. **courage** is to **courageous** as **outrage** is to _____

9. **commit** is to **commitment** as **equip** is to _____

10. **tell** is to **teller** as **propel** is to _____

11. **trace** is to **retraceable** as **place** is to _____

12. **personally** is to **impersonal** as **patiently** is to _____

13. **race** is to **racial** as **commerce** is to _____

14. **recur** is to **recurred** as **occur** is to _____

15. **legible** is to **illegible** as **responsible** is to _____

B. Complete each sentence with words from the spelling list.

1. The television show will begin _____ after the next _____ .

2. This informative _____ was a handy reference book during our tour.

3. No reputable newspaper _____ wants to be accused of _____ journalism.

4. The _____ didn't have _____ medical supplies to treat all victims of the _____ .

A. Find and circle the misspelled word in each row. Write it correctly.

1. adequately   impatient   oficial   _____
2. colapse   extravagance   competition   _____
3. physician   unikue   conquer   _____
4. inquisative   admitted   equipping   _____
5. regretted   replacable   enough   _____
6. reference   correspondant   occurrence   _____
7. propeller   labelling   difficult   _____
8. aquainted   catastrophe   immediately   _____
9. applicant   referred   atmospere   _____
10. occurred   outragous   irresponsible   _____
11. comercial   canceled   impatient   _____
12. equipment   pamplet   admittance   _____

B. Complete each analogy with a word from the list.

decipher	commentator	permitted	quarreled
pharmacy	catastrophe	affirmative	repel
enough	inquisitive	illuminate	connotation

1. **hard** is to **difficult** as **curious** is to   _____
2. **gently** is to **roughly** as **attract** is to   _____
3. **no** is to **yes** as **negative** is to   _____
4. **gain** is to **profit** as **meaning** is to   _____
5. **food** is to **grocery** as **medicine** is to   _____
6. **elegant** is to **fancy** as **sufficient** is to   _____
7. **language** is to **translate** as **code** is to   _____
8. **cease** is to **quit** as **enlighten** is to   _____
9. **newspaper** is to **columnist** as **television** is to   _____
10. **trembled** is to **quivered** as **argued** is to   _____
11. **movie** is to **entertainment** as **earthquake** is to   _____
12. **discussed** is to **conferred** as **allowed** is to   _____

Greek combining forms

Teaching

gram	gra<u>gram</u>mar	tele<u>gram</u>	*opti, opto*	<u>opti</u>cal	<u>opto</u>metry
phon	<u>phon</u>ics	tele<u>phon</u>e	*thermo*	<u>thermo</u>s	<u>thermo</u>meter
graph	<u>graph</u>ic	phono<u>graph</u>	*stat*	<u>stat</u>ic	thermo<u>stat</u>
naut	<u>naut</u>ical	astro<u>naut</u>	*typos*	<u>typ</u>ical	stereo<u>typ</u>e
meter, metry	<u>meter</u>	geo<u>metry</u>	*agon*	<u>agon</u>y	prot<u>agon</u>ist

Lesson Generalization: Combining forms are word elements that, unlike prefixes and suffixes, may be used in different positions when they are joined with other word elements.

Suffixes can be added to some **Greek combining forms** to make English nouns and adjectives:

> the noun suffix **ic** forms the noun **static:** stat + ic.
> the adjective suffix **cal** forms the adjective **optical:** opti + cal.

The spelling of the **Greek combining form** may change slightly when it is joined to other word parts: typos: typical.

Two **Greek combining forms** may be joined like the two parts of a compound word:

> night<u>time</u> / <u>time</u>keeper   tele<u>phone</u> / <u>phono</u>graph
> (compound words)   (Greek combining forms)

A. Complete the following exercises.

1. Greek combining forms can come at the beginning or end of a word—or both. Write the words from the word list in which the underlined Greek combining form comes at the beginning of the word.

_____   _____   _____

_____   _____   _____

_____   _____   _____

_____   _____

2. A Greek combining form can also be found in the middle of a word. Write the words from the word list in which the underlined Greek combining form is in the middle or at the end of the word.

_____   _____   _____

_____   _____   _____

_____   _____

B. On a separate sheet of paper use each word from the word list in an original sentence. Underline the list word in each.

Lesson 25 · Greek combining forms

More Practice

1. grammar	6. phonograph	11. optical	16. thermostat
2. telegram	7. nautical	12. optometry	17. typical
3. phonics	8. astronaut	13. thermos	18. stereotype
4. telephone	9. meter	14. thermometer	19. agony
5. graphic	10. geometry	15. static	20. protagonist

A. First look at the meanings of these Greek word parts. Then use the meaning of the Greek parts to find spelling words that match the definitions below.

tele – far
phon – sound
agon – contest, struggle
typos, typi – type
naut – sea, sailor

astro – star
thermo – heat
stat – stand
gram, graph – word,
    written or drawn

stere – strong
geo – earth
meter, metry – measure
opti, opto – vision

1. star sailor _____

2. heat-keeping device _____

3. rules for writing _____

4. profession measures
vision _____

5. strong type _____

6. words from afar _____

7. teaching of sounds _____

8. relating to vision _____

9. device carrying sound
from afar _____

10. science that measures
"earth angles" _____

11. serving as a type _____

12. relating to the sea _____

13. clearly drawn _____

14. instrument for drawing
sound _____

15. standing still _____

16. a painful struggle _____

17. unit of measure _____

18. device measures heat _____

19. one involved in a
struggle _____

20. device for keeping heat
at a standstill _____

B. Circle the word from each pair of spelling words that best completes the sentence.

1. (Grammar, Phonics) is the science of sound.

2. The reporter wrote a (static, graphic) description of the game.

3. Seeing a lake in a desert is a type of (optical, nautical) illusion.

4. Lower the (thermostat, thermometer) at night to save energy.

5. That (telegram, telephone) was delivered by (telegram, telephone).

Greek prefixes and combining forms

Lesson 26

Teaching

syn	+ thesis	= <u>syn</u>thesis	<u>thesis</u>	<u>chron</u>ic
syn	+ opsis	= <u>syn</u>opsis	hypo<u>thesis</u>	<u>chron</u>icle
syn	+ chron + ize	= <u>syn</u>chronize	paren<u>thesis</u>	<u>chron</u>ology
syn	+ metri +cal	= <u>sym</u>metrical		
syn	+ ptom	= <u>sym</u>ptom		
syn	+ pathy	= <u>sym</u>pathy	an<u>onym</u>ous	<u>path</u>ology
syn	+ bol	= <u>sym</u>bol	ant<u>onym</u>	a<u>path</u>y
syn	+ table	= <u>syl</u>lable	pseud<u>onym</u>	tele<u>path</u>y

Lesson Generalization: Greek prefixes, like Latin prefixes, may be assimilated into another word part. The spelling changes to make more compatible combinations:

in becomes **im** before **m**, **p**, **b**   **in** becomes **il** before **l**
syn becomes **sym** before **m**, **p**, **b**   **syn** becomes **syl** before **l**

Greek combining forms can be used in different ways to make English words.

They can be combined with a prefix: <u>**synonym**</u>; with a suffix: **chron<u>ic</u>, chron<u>icle</u>;** with a prefix and a suffix: **<u>synchronize</u>, <u>anonymous</u>;** or with another combining form: **<u>hypothesis</u>, <u>pseudonym</u>.**

A. Complete the following exercises.

1. Many Greek prefixes are assimilated into the word they join. Write the words from the spelling list that have the assimilated prefix **syn.**

   _____   _____   _____

   _____   _____   _____

   _____   _____

2. A Greek combining form sometimes comes at the beginning of a word. Write examples of these words from the spelling list.

   _____   _____   _____

   _____

3. A Greek combining form can also stand alone as a word or come at the middle or end of a word. Write examples of this type of word from the spelling list.

   _____   _____   _____

   _____   _____   _____

   _____   _____

B. On a separate sheet of paper, write a brief definition for each spelling word.

Greek prefixes and combining forms

More Practice

1. synthesis	6. sympathy	11. parenthesis	16. chronicle
2. synopsis	7. symbol	12. anonymous	17. chronology
3. synchronize	8. syllable	13. antonym	18. pathology
4. symmetrical	9. thesis	14. pseudonym	19. apathy
5. symptom	10. hypothesis	15. chronic	20. telepathy

A. Complete each sentence with a spelling word.

1. The school received a gift of money from an _____ donor.

2. The dove is a _____ of peace.

3. Let's _____ our watches before we separate.

4. Lack of attendance at the meeting was a sign of _____ among the students.

5. Mark Twain was a _____ for Samuel L. Clemens, who wrote *Tom Sawyer.*

6. The doctor said that a severe cough can be a _____ of several illnesses.

7. Our history book lists a _____ of the important events of the Civil War.

8. *Asymmetrical* is an _____ for *symmetrical.*

9. Is it possible to communicate by mental _____ ?

10. Put the accent mark on the second _____ of *pathology.*

11. Write a brief _____ , or summary, of the plot of the novel.

12. Can you arrange the flowers in a _____ design?

13. Asthma is a _____ disease.

14. We could show our _____ by helping the family left homeless by the fire.

15. A punctuation mark used to enclose or mark off a phrase in a sentence is called a

_____ .

16. The graduate student's _____ was due at the end of the term.

17. The scientist's _____ was found untrue.

B. On a separate sheet of paper write five sentences, one for each spelling word not used in exercise A.

Lesson 27 Latin and Greek Plurals

Teaching

memorandum	memorandums	(memoranda)
radius	radii	(radiuses)
curriculum	curricula	(curriculums)
criterion	criteria	(criterions)
index	indexes	(indeces)
appendix	appendixes	(appendices)
octopus	octopuses	(octopi)
aquarium	aquariums	(aquaria)
stadium	stadiums	(stadia)
vacuum	vacuums	(vacua)
medium	media	(medias)

datum	data	crisis	crises
agendum	agenda	oasis	oases
		basis	bases
stimulus	stimuli	diagnosis	diagnoses
alumnus	alumni	analysis	analyses

Lesson Generalization: Some words still use only the Latin or Greek plural forms. A few of these have an alternative English plural. For other words, the English plural form is preferred. Because these kinds of language changes are gradual, older dictionaries may have different information than more recent dictionaries. Common usage has almost eliminated the Latin singular of some words, such as **datum** and **agendum**.

A. Complete the following exercises.

1. Which two Latin words in the word list rarely appear in their singular form?

   _____   _____

2. Write the preferred plural spelling for all words in the list.

   _____   _____   _____

   _____   _____   _____

   _____   _____   _____

   _____   _____   _____

   _____   _____   _____

   _____   _____

B. On a separate sheet of paper alphabetize the plural forms of the words in the list.

Latin and Greek Plurals

Lesson 27

More Practice

1. crises	6. stimuli	11. indexes	16. vacuums
2. bases	7. alumni	12. appendixes	17. memorandums
3. oases	8. radii	13. octopuses	18. data
4. diagnoses	9. curricula	14. aquariums	19. media
5. analyses	10. criteria	15. stadiums	20. agendas

A. Write the preferred plural form of each word listed below.

1. vacuum _____
2. octopus _____
3. medium _____
4. appendix _____
5. aquarium _____
6. stimulus _____
7. memorandum _____

8. crisis _____
9. radius _____
10. basis _____
11. alumnus _____
12. curriculum _____
13. agenda _____
14. analysis _____

B. Write the plural forms of the spelling words that match the clues and fit the puzzle.

Across

2. doctor's opinion
5. eight-armed creature
8. prod to action
11. standard for judging
12. extra matter at book's end
13. school graduate
14. desert green spot

Down

1. foundation
3. outdoor arena
4. fish tank
6. course of study
7. line from the center of circle to its edge
9. alphabetical list of contents
10. information, facts

The prefix *ex*

Teaching

ex + ception = exception	ex + amine = examine	
ex + citement = excitement	ex + asperate = exasperate	
ex + cellent = excellent	ex + aggerate = exaggerate	
ex + ceed = exceed	ex + act = exact	
ex + cerpt = excerpt	ex + ercise = exercise	
	ex + ertion = exertion	
ex + hausted = exhausted	ex + emption = exemption	
ex + hibited = exhibited	ex + istence = existence	
ex + hale = exhale	ex + ile = exile	
	ex + it = exit	
	ex + ample = example	
	ex + ecutive = executive	

Lesson Generalization: Only a few words in the English language are formed by adding **ex** to a soft **c** or to the letter **h**. No words are formed by adding **ex** to the letter **s** or the letter **z**. The sound of /**s**/ or /**z**/ is made by the **x** in the prefix **ex.**

The prefix **ex** is added directly to many roots beginning with vowels. The spelling of the prefix does not change when it is joined to vowels or to the letters **c** or **h.**

A. Complete the following exercises.

1. The prefix **ex** does not change when added to roots beginning with _____ or the letters **c** or **h.** Write examples of list words formed by joining **ex** to a root beginning with a vowel.

   _____   _____   _____

   _____   _____   _____

   _____   _____   _____

   _____   _____   _____

2. Write examples of list words in which the prefix **ex** comes before a root beginning with **c** or **h.**

   _____   _____   _____

   _____   _____   _____

   _____   _____

B. On a separate sheet of paper, write a story of the "exes." Use at least 12 "ex" words from the list in your story. Have fun with this exercise. Share your work with a few classmates.

Lesson 28 **The prefix *ex*** *More Practice*

1. exception 6. exhausted 11. exaggerate 16. existence
2. excitement 7. exhibited 12. exact 17. exile
3. excellent 8. exhale 13. exercise 18. exit
4. exceed 9. examine 14. exertion 19. example
5. excerpt 10. exasperate 15. exemption 20. executive

A. The words **exact, exercise, exile,** and **exit** each have several meaning. Read a dictionary entry for each of these words. Then complete each of the following sentences with one of the words. You may need to add endings.

1. Are you going to attend the graduation _____ tonight?

2. The hero's dramatic _____ comes at the end of the first act.

3. Give the clerk the _____ amount of change.

4. The basketball team _____ daily to keep in shape.

5. We should _____ quietly and quickly during a fire drill.

6. My neighbor is an _____ from his native country.

7. The scoutmaster recommends that we _____ caution when hiking.

8. That government may _____ the rebel from the country.

9. The trainer must _____ obedience from the animals she works with.

10. Complete this math _____ for homework.

B. Circle the 12 words from the spelling list that are hidden in this word search puzzle. They are written forward, backward, up, and down.

D	T	E	C	N	E	T	S	I	X	E	E
D	Q	X	C	T	X	P	V	X	N	X	L
E	B	E	Y	N	E	R	E	K	O	H	A
T	X	M	M	E	C	E	X	D	I	I	H
S	D	P	H	L	U	C	A	E	T	B	X
U	V	T	J	L	T	X	M	E	P	I	E
A	Q	I	R	E	I	E	I	C	E	T	N
H	W	O	Z	C	V	V	N	X	C	E	J
X	F	N	W	X	E	T	E	E	X	D	F
E	T	A	R	E	P	S	A	X	E	I	X

Lesson 29 Paired prefixes

Teaching

mis + stated = misstated	ad + tain = attain
un + stated = unstated	com + tain = contain
dis + sect = dissect	ex + fort = effort
in + sect = insect	com + fort = comfort
com + motion = commotion	com + lection = collection
de + motion = demotion	ex + lection = election
ad + cent = accent	com + laborate = collaborate
re + cent = recent	ex + laborate = elaborate
ad + cess = access	com + rosion = corrosion
re + cess = recess	ex + rosion = erosion

Lesson Generalization: Some double consonants occur because the last letter of the prefix is the same as the first letter of the base word or root: misstated.

Most double consonants occur because the prefix is assimilated. The last letter of the prefix changes to match the first letter of the base word or root: ad + cent = accent.

Remember that one of the double consonants belongs to the prefix, and one belongs to the root or base word.

A. Complete the following exercises.

1. In some words, a prefix is added to a root or base word without a change in spelling. A double consonant results when the last letter of the prefix matches the first letter of the root or base. Write all words from the list that do not change the spelling of the root or prefix when a prefix is added.

   _____ _____ _____

   _____ _____ _____

   _____ _____ _____

2. In many words, the prefix is assimilated—it changes spelling when added to the root or base word. Write the words from the list that have assimilated prefixes.

   _____ _____ _____

   _____ _____ _____

   _____ _____ _____

   _____ _____

B. On a separate sheet of paper, write each pair of words from the word list. Then make a new word by joining a new prefix to the root or base of each pair.

Paired prefixes

More Practice

1. misstated	6. demotion	11. attain	16. election
2. unstated	7. accent	12. contain	17. collaborate
3. dissect	8. recent	13. effort	18. elaborate
4. insect	9. access	14. comfort	19. corrosion
5. commotion	10. recess	15. collection	20. erosion

A. Complete each sentence with two spelling words that have the same root.

1. The major's _____ in rank caused a great _____ among other officers.

2. Your foreign _____ reveals that you are a _____ arrival to this country.

3. She had _____ her feelings in the past, so now she left her opinions

    _____ .

4. Phil and Lou plan to _____ on an _____ science project.

5. I could not _____ my happiness when I saw we would _____ our goal.

6. Chemical _____ resulted in the _____ of the metal.

7. Each student will _____ an _____ in science class today.

8. Lee prefers to rest in _____ rather than exert any _____ .

9. Ruth started a _____ of posters and buttons from the presidential

    _____ .

10. Students have _____ to the gym at the noon _____ .

B. Make spelling words from these sets of words. First cross out one letter in each word. Then write the remaining letters together to form a spelling word.

1. rinse + act = _____   9. be + labors + fate = _____

2. corn + tap + pin = _____   10. arc + cents = _____

3. hero + sit + ton = _____   11. mist + stay + tend = _____

4. demon + tin + won = _____ 12. colt + slab + ornate = _____

5. are + aces + so = _____   13. disk + use + cat = _____

6. fun + state + red = _____ 14. bat + tap + ink = _____

7. cold + elect + ions = _____ 15. sac + cress = _____

8. are + cents = _____   16. cord + rose + in + son = _____

Lesson 30 Words from the French language

r<u>ou</u>te	rest<u>au</u>rant
r<u>ou</u>ge	ch<u>au</u>ffeur
c<u>ou</u>pon	ch<u>au</u>vinist
t<u>ou</u>rist	
g<u>ou</u>rmet	l<u>ie</u>utenant
p<u>ou</u>ltry	sold<u>ie</u>r
s<u>ou</u>venir	chandel<u>ie</u>r
b<u>ou</u>levard	
car<u>ou</u>sel	sur<u>geon</u>
lim<u>ou</u>sine	dun<u>geon</u>
silh<u>ou</u>ette	pi<u>geon</u>

Lesson Generalization: Spelling follows certain patterns in every language. The vowel combinations **ou**, **au**, and **ie** occur in many words taken from the French language. The **ou** combination most frequently appears in a first syllable.

Only words from the French use the **geon** ending. They cause spelling challenges because the **ge** in words such as **surgeon** sounds like the **dge** in English words: fu<u>dge</u>, ju<u>dge</u>.

A. Complete the following exercises.

1. Three common letter combinations in French are **ou, au,** and **ie.** These combinations also appear in French words that have been adopted into the English language. Write words from the spelling list that have the **ou** combination.

_____   _____   _____

_____   _____   _____

_____   _____   _____

_____   _____

2. Write the spelling words with the **au** letter combination.

_____   _____   _____

3. Write the spelling words with the **ie** letter combination.

_____   _____

4. What three words have the French **geon** ending?

_____   _____   _____

B. On a separate sheet of paper, write a "French" story. Use at least 12 words from the spelling list. Share your story with a partner.

Lesson 30 Words from the French language

1. route	6. poultry	11. silhouette	16. soldier
2. rouge	7. souvenir	12. restaurant	17. chandelier
3. coupon	8. boulevard	13. chauffeur	18. surgeon
4. tourist	9. carousel	14. chauvinist	19. dungeon
5. gourmet	10. limousine	15. lieutenant	20. pigeon

A. Write an answer for each question, using one of the spelling words. The underlined words in the questions will help you decide which words to use.

1. Is he a <u>visitor</u> from Japan?

_____

2. Do you have a discount <u>ticket</u>?

_____

3. Is Mr. Anders an <u>excellent judge of fine foods</u>?

_____

4. Can the artist draw an <u>outline</u> of your face?

_____

5. Are there many <u>chicken</u> recipes in the cookbook?

_____

6. Did the actress apply more <u>make-up</u> before she went on stage?

_____

7. Did you bring home a <u>remembrance</u> from your trip?

_____

8. Is the <u>driver of the limousine</u> experienced?

_____

9. Does the crystal in the <u>light fixture</u> come from Italy?

_____

10. Would you describe her <u>as an overly opinionate person</u>?

_____

B. On a seperate sheet of paper, write an original sentence for all the words not used in A.

Lesson 31 **Pronunciation problems** *Teaching*

gen<u>e</u>ral	dec<u>i</u>mal	post<u>p</u>one	recognize
sev<u>e</u>ral	priv<u>i</u>lege	quan<u>ti</u>ty	hand<u>s</u>ome
int<u>e</u>rest	choc<u>o</u>late	e<u>t</u> cetera	bu<u>d</u>get
prob<u>a</u>bly	soph<u>o</u>more	enviro<u>n</u>ment	ki<u>t</u>chen
gard<u>e</u>ner	fav<u>o</u>rite	gover<u>n</u>ment	whis<u>t</u>le

Lesson Generalization: An unstressed middle vowel is sometimes dropped when the word is pronounced. The three-syllable word seems to shrink to a two-syllable word:

gen-er-al sounds like **gen-ral**   **fav-or-ite** sounds like **fav-rite**

Certain consonant combinations do not blend together smoothly: **tp, nm, gn**. One of the consonants may accidentally be dropped when the word is pronounced.

gover-ment instead of **government**
reco-nize instead of **recognize**
pos-pone instead of **postpone**

In some other words, the difficult consonant is retained in the spelling but is never pronounced: ki<u>t</u>chen; whis<u>t</u>le

A. Complete the following exercises.

1. Some words are difficult to spell because they have a consonant in the middle that is not pronounced. Write four examples of this type of word from the list.

   _____   _____   _____   _____

   _____

2. Some other words are difficult to spell because consonant combinations such as **tp, mn** and **gn** do not blend well. Write six examples from the word list.

   _____   _____   _____

   _____   _____   _____

3. An unstressed middle vowel is often dropped when a word is pronounced. This vowel is often also forgotten when the word is spelled. Write ten examples of this type of word from the word list.

   _____   _____   _____

   _____   _____   _____

   _____   _____   _____

   _____

B. On a separate sheet of paper, write the words from the word list in alphabetical order.

Lesson 31 Pronunciation problems

More Practice

1. general	6. decimal	11. postpone	16. recognize
2. several	7. privilege	12. quantity	17. handsome
3. interest	8. chocolate	13. et cetera	18. budget
4. probably	9. sophomore	14. environment	19. kitchen
5. gardener	10. favorite	15. government	20. whistle

A. Write the spelling word that contains the smaller word. Do not repeat any spelling words in this exercise.

1. his _____

2. rite _____

3. one _____

4. den _____

5. over _____

6. rest _____

7. ever _____

8. hen _____

9. rob _____

10. more _____

11. vile _____

12. cog _____

13. and _____

14. era _____

15. ant _____

16. iron _____

17. get _____

18. late _____

B. Fill in the blanks with words from the spelling list. Use each word once.

1. Did you hear the teapot _____ from the stove in the _____ ?

2. My brother's _____ year in high school was his _____ year.

3. The federal _____ plays a major role in protecting the _____ .

4. I hardly _____ you, you look so _____ in your tuxedo!

5. Sara considers it a great _____ to eat fine _____ from Switzerland.

6. Tim got _____ math problems wrong because he forgot the _____ points.

7. The _____ of CDs you buy will have an effect on your _____ .

8. The new movie will _____ _____ you because you love sad stories.

9. I usually _____ chores, homework, _____ if I can.

10. One _____ career I would like to investigate is that of being a _____ .

Review

Lesson 32

1. grammar	9. crises	17. exceed	25. restaurant
2. typical	10. indexes	18. collection	26. surgeon
3. astronaut	11. diagnoses	19. commotion	27. et cetera
4. thermometer	12. stadiums	20. collaborate	28. privilege
5. chronic	13. exaggerate	21. accent	29. government
6. symptom	14. exercise	22. route	30. recognize
7. anonymous	15. excellent	23. coupon	
8. syllable	16. exhausted	24. souvenir	

A. Complete each analogy with a word from the spelling list.

1. **elect** is to **election** as **collect** is to _____

2. **equip** is to **equipment** as **govern** is to _____

3. **oasis** is to **oases** as **crisis** is to _____

4. **inc.** is to **incorporated** as **etc.** is to _____

5. **examination** is to **examine** as **exaggeration** is to _____

6. **elect** is to **elaborate** as **collect** is to _____

7. **graphic** is to **phonograph** as **nautical** is to _____

8. **promise** is to **compromise** as **motion** is to _____

9. **intelligence** is to **intelligent** as **excellence** is to _____

10. **aquarium** is to **aquariums** as **stadium** is to _____

11. **coupons** is to **coupon** as **souvenirs** is to _____

12. **exhibition** is to **exhibited** as **exhaustion** is to _____

13. **organization** is to **organize** as **recognition** is to _____

14. **analyze** is to **analyses** as **diagnose** is to _____

15. **appendix** is to **appendixes** as **index** is to _____

B. Complete each sentence with words from the spelling list.

1. Susan clipped the _____ for a meal at the new _____ .

2. Is the _____ on the first or the second _____ in that word?

3. If you _____ the speed limit, you may lose the _____ of driving.

4. The latest _____ letter is a _____ example of the writer's poor _____ .

5. The _____ measured Karen's fever.

Review

Lesson 32

A. Three words in each row follow the same spelling pattern. Circle the word that does not follow the pattern.

1. nautical   telephone   astronaut   thermometer

2. exception   excuse   exceed   excellent

3. contain   kitchen   whistle   sophomore

4. commotion   corrosion   comfort   collection

5. synonym   symptom   anonymous   pseudonym

6. crises   bases   diagnoses   recesses

7. budget   dungeon   surgeon   pigeon

8. misstated   dissect   unstated   access

9. chauffeur   analysis   silhouette   chauvinist

10. stimulus   alumnus   vacuum   curriculum

B. Complete each analogy with a word from the list.

synopsis   symbol   chocolate   poultry   exaggerate
carousel   octopus   chauffeur   erosion   optical
aquarium   oasis   pseudonym   antonym   sophomore

1. **same** is to **opposite** as **synonym** is to _____

2. **lion** is to **zoo** as **fish** is to _____

3. **junior** is to **senior** as **freshman** is to _____

4. **sea** is to **nautical** as **eye** is to _____

5. **sour** is to **lemon** as **sweet** is to _____

6. **ham** is to **pork** as **chicken** is to _____

7. **one hundred** is to **centipede** as **eight** is to _____

8. **car** is to **driver** as **limousine** is to _____

9. **metal** is to **corrosion** as **soil** is to _____

10. **patriotism** is to **flag** as **idea** is to _____

11. **ocean** is to **island** as **desert** is to _____

12. **watch** is to **clock** as **merry-go-round** is to _____

13. **simile** is to **compare** as **hyperbole** is to _____

14. **composition** is to **essay** as **summary** is to _____

15. **Samuel Clemens** is to **Mark Twain** as **name** is to _____